Authorities Comment on *Survivors of Predator Priests*

Jim Handlin's *Survivors of Predator Priests* delivers a gripping journey into the lives of victims and their families, and the controversial issue of clergy sexual abuse. While much has been written about offenders and the Catholic Church, few works have succeeded in revealing the horrors of abuse and its long-lasting impacts through the eyes of the survivor. This book accomplishes the task in a manner that is thoughtful and genuine.

The survivors' personal narratives show how abuser priests hide behind a mask of trust and popularity to gain power and access in the lives of children and their families. The dynamic of why victims remain silent for years is illuminated poignantly, as is their quest to achieve peace and justice.

This book represents an important element of clergy abuse crisis, and is a must read for those questioning religion, power, and accountability.

Susan M. Archibald, President
The Linkup—Survivors of Clergy Abuse

Jim Handlin has catalogued the trauma of clergy sexual molestation that has enveloped the Catholic Church throughout the last seventy-five years of her history in the United States. This tale is unique. The collection of stories that Jim Handlin has tapped together into a mosaic of criminal conspiracy is told tile-by-tile from the perspective of the individual survivor. Each story holds the truth of the experience of both the devastating horror of sexual abuse, rape, and sodomy, as well as the responses that the survivor received (or did not receive) from church leaders.

This book is, in effect, not only a chronicle of the expected difficulties encountered by sex crime victims (dealing with intimacy/sex and depression, for example), but also a coldly illustrated tabulation of broken family relationships, damaged trust in one's parents and other authority figures, and lost faith in the church and, more importantly, even in

God. Jim Handlin exposes the truth of the clergy molestation scandal with extreme sadness and tenderness.

The power of this communal story lay in the revelation of secrets that have been kept hidden by each individual for years; in some cases, decades. The brave men and women who unveil their pain, suffering, and shame in these pages have given us a generous gift. They have grafted flesh, tissue, and muscle to the masks of the thousands of survivors who have reported their abuse to law enforcement leaders and church leaders, and for too many, only to be turned away with sanctimonious derision and indifference toward the human condition.

Undaunted, survivors continue to overcome their pain and embarrassment to put a human face on their stories of shame and suffering, all the while shedding light on the evil each has experienced at the hands of trusted clergy. Their doing so benefits the Church with the singular gifts of charity of purpose and hope for the future.

Only by exposing these dark deeds can the church begin the necessary and arduous task of healing herself. Readers of Handlin's history of the American church also must recognize that even though he only is able to share the experiences of eight survivors, the truth documented herein encapsulates and validates the stories of thousands of others who have been sexually molested in the same manner. Whether the abuse occurred one time, or several times a week for several years, the innocence that was shattered and the consequences brought about in the lives of the victims, their families, and their parish and school communities has been devastating.

In so many ways, the survivors of clergy sexual abuse have become the "wounded healers" of the church. The great Dutch teacher and pastoral care specialist Henri J. M. Nouwen notes: "When we honestly ask ourselves which persons in our lives mean the most to us, we often find that it is those who, instead of giving advice, solutions, or cures, have chosen rather to share our pain and touch our wounds with a warm and tender hand."

This woundedness of shattered faith in humanity and, yes, God (vis-à-vis Church as authority and as institution) demands this level of response. Almost all, if not all, survivors have experienced this loss of trust and faith in varying degrees.

The lack of understanding and poor response has shaped what has become, perhaps, a significant hallmark of many of us molested by a priest, nun, or a professed religious: speaking out courageously, a hundred times over if necessary, until our story is heard. Identifying the criminal sexual predator, especially those still in ministry today, not only nurtures the healing process; it also removes all potential risk to untold numbers of additional innocent children. The church will continue to be haunted by the evil of sacrificing the vulnerable and young for the gratification of church leaders with perverse appetites, but those who tell their stories and expose the truth today know that they have established a firm foundation for a renewed life and a recovering faith.

Jim Handlin's documentation represents a decisive and damning moment in the history of the Roman Catholic Church. With the help of survivors, he reveals the total lack of desire of church leaders to confront and accept these atrocities as they occurred. Their stories expose the consequences and "fall-out" of the abuse of children and vulnerable adults beyond what one would expect. Handlin has, in fact, distilled and refined raw nuggets of painful truth as told by survivors of sexual molestation by spiritual leaders. Too many survivors have been left alone, treated as the "enemy" of God and the Church rather than as a community of humble witnesses—teachers, if you will—of the unbridled corruption of temporal and spiritual power in this mournful era of the Catholic Church in America. Handlin has exposed the failed leadership of the church and the need to create a better, more helpful, environment for survivors and family members. But few of us (or, perhaps, none) have really been told that our courage in coming forward is appreciated or even recognized by those who should have been our friends. Consequently, many, who read these pages, will find the subject matter intimidating, overwhelming, or even depressing. But I hope you will soon understand that this book is fundamentally about strength and courage. Storytelling demands a powerful, unique voice. Handlin and those who have generously offered us this genuine gift of the heart have exposed the evil of clergy sexual abuse for what it truly is: the abuse of power and authority within the Catholic Church. These "children," and thousand more like them, have chosen to survive and even thrive. Others, sadly, have chosen surrender, lacking the fortitude and hope necessary for survival. But by choosing to fight for healing, honesty, and prevention, in spite of all we have endured, perhaps those unable to cope will be able to rediscover their resolve and move forward.

In our dozens of SNAP self-help groups across the country, we often repeat one of our ground rules: "Take what you like, leave the rest. Cling to what you find helpful here, let everything else go." I urge you to do that with this book. Some chapters will resonate and touch you. Others may not. But collectively, there is much wisdom in the pages ahead for every reader.

Thank you for picking up this book. Thank you for taking the time to address this painful topic. I hope you will join with me, too, in thanking each of the contributors who so selflessly and bravely shared his or her own experiences, so that others might learn, heal, and prevent future harm to innocent kids and vulnerable adults!

Barbara A. Blaine, President
Survivors Network of those Abused by Priests (SNAP)

The voices of survivors of clergy sexual abuse have finally been raised, but the newspapers don't tell the whole story. Even if one is aware of this storm raging against the Roman Catholic Church, one may not truly understand what it means. For that, it takes the stories of the victims themselves, told in their own words. Though each tale is different, each has certain similarities to all others.

Everything in these stories from how the victim is groomed to how the perpetrator uses the system to keep perpetrating will sound eerily familiar to survivors and their families, as will the accounts of the devastation that results.

For them, some of the stories here may be hard to take, but it is for others who have not been there that these accounts may have the most value.

Authorities Comment on *Survivors of Predator Priests*

Because it is important to note that by and large these are not momentary crimes of passion, where the clerical perpetrator is overwhelmed by mad temptation. These are felonies calculated well in advance, audaciously committed, and confidently covered up. The courage of these survivors to finally speak out each in his or her own way, sometimes after decades of silence and denial, is therefor greater, and also evident here.

This book is a testament to that courage, and to their resolve to expose the predatory wolves in clerical collars in our midst.

Jay Nelson, Author The Harrowing

The survivors's story of sexual abuse is not an easy story to read. But it is an even harder story to live. Catholics, and all people of good will, need to read the stories in this book.

The men and women who have written these chapters share their memories of the events and experiences of innocent young people who, years later, recall the vivid details of their abuse.

In reading these stories, I hope that readers will reflect more deeply, and more carefully, about the injustice done to thousands of children, adolescents, and young adults. Why did these terrible events take place? What power allowed this to happen? Women, as well as men, have been victims of abuse. Their stories are here as well as those of boys and young men. All of these stories need to be read.

We are still a long way from understanding the sociology and the psychology surrounding sexual abuse. These first-hand accounts will help us develop that understanding. They will not comfort us. But in our discomfort, we may doing ourselves, and thousands of children, the greatest favor.

By vowing to never again trust men in power who are unaccountable for their actions, we will prove to survivors that we have understood the message of their stories. They are the living witnesses of terrible abuse. We must become the witnesses of commitment that such abuse will not happen again.

Jim Post, President, Voice of the Faithful

Survivors of Predator Priests

Survivors
of
Predator Priests

Edited by

J. M. Handlin

TAPESTRY PRESS
IRVING, TEXAS

Tapestry Press
3649 Conflans Road
Suite 103
Irving, TX 75061

Printed in the U.S.A.

09 08 07 06 05   1 2 3 4 5

Library of Congress Cataloging-in-Publication Data

Survivors of predator priests / edited by J.M. Handlin.
    p. cm.
  Summary: "Eight men and women recount their childhood experiences of
being sexually abused by Roman Catholic priests and they discuss the impact
that abuse has had on their lives"--Provided by publisher.
  ISBN-10: 1-930819-42-0 (trade paper : alk. paper)
  ISBN-13: 978-1-930819-42-9
  1. Catholic Church--United States--Clergy--Sexual behavior. 2. Child sexual
abuse by clergy--United States. 3. Sexual abuse victims--United States. I.
Handlin, J. M. (James Monroe), 1941-
  BX1912.9.S87 2005
  261.8'3272'088282--dc22

                              2004028364

Cover and book design and layout by
D. & F. Scott Publishing, Inc.
N. Richland Hills, Texas

Dedicated to

all who have been sexually abused and molested by Catholic priests, many of whom have been unable to come forward. It is hoped this book will help them realize they are not alone, the abuse was not their fault, they should have no guilt or shame associated with the abuse they suffered, and help them begin or continue their healing process.

Contents

Foreword

Father Thomas Doyle, O.P., J.C.D.

The Roman Catholic clergy sex abuse phenomenon that has unfolded like a deadly cloud over church and society is, without a doubt, the worst example of the Church gone awry since the Inquisition. Unlike the Inquisition, however, the victims of this nightmare will not be consigned to anonymous oblivion. Many of the thousands who have had their bodies and their souls violated by members of the clerical elite have emerged from the depressive and defeating pit of victimhood to become survivors. Though used and often cast aside by the uncaring and callous official ministers of the Church, these men and women have refused to stay beaten down and have risen to challenge the ecclesiastical institution and the society that has stood too often silent and complicit.

The survivors of Catholic clergy sexual abuse are unlike any other sexual abuse victims. In an interview with the National Catholic Reporter in August, 2003, Dr. Leslie Lothstein, of the Institute for the Living, characterized the impact of sexual abuse by a priest as "soul murder" and so it is. The priest, as Catholics are taught from their earliest years, takes the place of Christ. When a devout and unquestioning believer is violated by a priest, the shock penetrates to the depths of the soul. The victim experiences a unique kind of despondence because he or she feels betrayed by one who has been trusted even more than a parent, and even worse, abandoned by the God personified by the abusing cleric.

The utterly remarkable thing about the survivors, including those whose stories are told in this book, is that they are able to rise above their spiritual devastation, emerging as strong and focused advocates for the Truth. If any aspect of this entire debacle reflects the work of the true Spirit of God, it is the often incredible resilience of survivors.

Their stories tell much more than sordid tales of clerical betrayal with the consequent soul rape and murder. They take us to a deeper understanding of the dark side of organized religion and certainly the dark side of institutional Catholicism. We see the terrible consequences of the irrational power that clerics hold over countless believers—a power grounded in their self-styled exalted role as essential intermediary between the distant and often stern God, and the helpless sheeplike lay folk. This power, which the victims are taught never to question, helps forge what psychologists have labeled the "trauma bond." This bond explains why victims are all too often powerless to stop a repeating clergy predator who abuses again and again, each time dragging his prey even deeper into the pit of despair. This same bond is the reason why so many wait in fear for years or even decades before coming into the light to publicly name their abuse and the abuser.

The survivors' stories reveal a pathetically inept and traitorous hierarchical superstructure that was so consumed by its own self-concept and controlled by its addiction to power that it was and remains blinded to the horrendous rape and pillage going on in its very midst. The reaction to the betrayal by the hierarchy has been not only understandable anger and fury, but also a surprising and encouraging spiritual maturation of not only the survivors but an ever increasing number of lay people and even a small number of priests. They are coming forward and shedding the chains of clericalist oppression and laying claim to their right to be true members of the Church and not just silent and docile fund sources, treated as if they were all four years old.

The survivors of clergy sex abuse have "survived" much more than the assaults on their bodies. They have survived spiritual devastation and religious slavery that has kept the vast majority of the Catholic Church's membership locked in a spiritual time warp from which they were not allowed to venture past late infancy.

The survivors are a unique group. They have suffered intensely. They have been betrayed by the clergy and the Church they trusted without question. They have emerged as prophets, pointing the way to a healthier and more authentic church . . . a church that is walking out of the dark shadows of the medieval museum into the light of the Body of Christ.

Sonia's Story

Editor's Comments

Sonia was first abused at the young age of eight. The abusive priest, who was reading from the Bible to her, reached down and pulled her panties down, and inserted his fingers into her vagina. She was unable to cope with this invasion of her body. She could not resist or argue, and consequently she did nothing. This is understandable for such a young child and also typical of the reaction of other survivors when they were abused.

This follows, unfortunately, a common pattern. A young Catholic child is sexually abused but has no way of resisting. After all, they have been told by their parents that the priests are holy and God's representatives. What the priests tell them in confession is not to be revealed to anyone, even their parents. So the idea that a child can have a secret involving the priest and not tell their parents is ingrained in Catholic children from their first Holy Communion when they make their first confession.

Sonia was also told by the abusive priest that, if she told anyone what the priest was doing to her, God would take her parents. Someone she loved would die. Sonia was terrified, and could not risk losing some member of her family.

Jennifer was also facing this same threat from the Monsignor who sexually abused her for four years. As she says, she was protecting her mother to a great extent.

My maiden name, and my name at the time of the abuse, was Sonia Elizabeth Zelayandia. My married name is Sonia Elizabeth Todd. It is important to me that anyone reading my story knows my name.

My first interview for this book was on 19 February, 2003, as Jim Handlin and I sat watching the Pacific Ocean near the San Francisco Zoo. Here is my story, as it happened.

I lived for a long time, being alone and unheard, keeping all the emotions from my childhood to myself. The Church talks about Hell and Purgatory: I was in sheer hell for years.

Just talking to SNAP (Survivors Network of those Abused by Priests), and attending the SNAP meetings has been so healing for me. It helped to know there were others like me that have experienced this tremendous crime. At the same time, I was sad, realizing there were other victims. I believed for a long time I was the only one to have survived this horrible experience.

My abuse was not to be talked about within my family. The subject could not even be brought up. Not to be able to speak about something so important to my life, not to be heard with compassion, has been grueling for me. So I thank you very much for writing our stories. They need to be heard.

I am not telling you my story to seek pity, but to present the truth. People need to hear the truth about sexual abuse by priests. I want to encourage other survivors, whether in Latin America or anywhere in the world, to come forth and make their voices heard. If even one person comes forward because of my story, then I will have done what I came into this world to do.

I no longer see myself as a survivor, but as a thriver, a person who has been to a place of darkness and risen above it. Because of my rising above this darkness, perhaps I can teach others how they can also rise above evil.

I wanted to say that much. Now I will close my eyes for a moment and then take you to that first initial violation.

I was eight years old and going to catechism every week. My first communion was coming up soon. My younger sister would also go to the church with me. The catechism class was taught by a nun—a mean old nun.

There were other ladies, usually mothers, who would help with the class. My grandmother, my mother's mother, would walk us there. Sometimes our nanny would take us, because we were too young to go alone.

It amazes me that, every time I talk about this or go back and explain what my experiences have been, it is still so painful. At the same time, I know now that I am not alone and that I didn't bring this on myself. I know I didn't cause it and I know I am not responsible for it. As I tell my story, I know that Christopher, my husband, is here for me, as well as my two children, Amy and Mark. I know who I am. And I am here for Little Sonia.

On this particular day, we were being taught different prayers. We needed to memorize them, and I was having trouble. It was boring and repetitive and didn't make sense to me. I couldn't grasp the meaning of what I was being told to memorize. The nun would get mad and hit my hands with her ruler, as if that would somehow give a boost to my brain and help me memorize the prayers, right?

It might not have taught me how to memorize, but it did teach me the power of the nuns. They were much more powerful than me. During the catechism classes, they inflicted pain on me, as if that was a measurement of my understanding. That still causes me pain when I think back to those classes. The pain certainly didn't make me any smarter.

There was a priest who wanted to be called Padre Carlitos. His name is Carlos Villacorta.

Padre Carlitos, or Father Charlie in English, walked into the class just as I was being disciplined. He stopped the nun from hitting my hands, and told her my mother had given him permission to take me to the rectory. He was going to teach me other ways to learn the prayers and my catechism. Now I believe that was a lie, about my mother giving her permission for him to take me out of class, but at the time I did not question it, and neither did the nun.

Padre Carlitos was always smiling and shaking the kids' hands. Some of the older ladies would come out and kiss his hand. He could have been my oldest brother, or my uncle, someone like that. He represented someone I could trust, so I didn't have any fear or mistrust of going with him. I had full confidence in him. Any sense of mistrust or any lack of trust was not in my psyche.

When he asked me to go with him, I didn't argue. I let him take my hand and lead me away from the nuns and the other students. I didn't call out to my grandmother to save me. I had no feeling of fear at all, just complete trust, as if I had gone with my father or my brother or even my dog. This was someone I totally trusted.

He took me behind this huge altar in the church. I heard him whistle to another priest, an older man, who could have been my great grandfather. Father Carlitos whistled to this older man and the older man whistled back. I was not concerned about the whistles, I was just there with this priest. I never wondered what the whistling was all about. The older man carried a large bunch of keys that seemed to signify he worked for the Church.

Father Carlitos told me what he was going to do. He looked straight at me. He said, "I want you to know that God has told me what to do with you." I was thinking about the lessons. I thought maybe I would be coloring or painting, something along the lines of learning a shortcut to catechism.

Then the priest told me that I should feel proud because God had selected me from a group of children for the actions he was about to perform. "La Novia." He was prepping me for what was coming. I was feeling uplifted and proud, having been selected as the wife, the girlfriend of God, which is what "La Novia" means. To be the girlfriend of God. This is a sublime place to be. I was feeling the pride of being selected from among the other children, not knowing what was coming next.

He picked up the Bible from a small table holding the holy water and opened it up and started to read. Next he reached his hand over toward me and pulled me a little closer. As I was standing next to him, he put his hand under my dress and pulled my panties down. He picked up the Bible and started reading a passage aloud. As he was reading the Bible, he put his finger into my vagina and kept thrusting his finger into me.

At that moment I felt shame. I didn't know what that feeling was before he did that to me. He told me God had chosen me for all the things he was going to do with me. He told me I was a sinner, because I was allowing him to do these things. At the same time, he told me I should be proud of what he has done, but I was still a sinner.

This was totally unexpected. I had no way of dealing with this physical, spiritual, and sexual abuse except to stand there motionless.

I wanted to leave the church and go back to where the other children were, back to safety, where no one would touch me. I looked over and saw the other man was watching us. I didn't understand what was happening. I think that day I died. My heart just broke into millions of pieces.

I was feeling all of these emotions. Silently screaming for help, praying for an earthquake, and praying for someone to walk in and save me. Yet there was someone already there, watching us. The old priest was there watching, but he didn't do or say anything. He didn't save me, so I swallowed all the emotions inside of me because I was too young to understand what was happening.

After some minutes had passed, he pulled my panties up and smoothed my dress. He told me that I had liked it and it was my fault that he had done that because I wore my little dress too short and my legs were too pretty. I must have liked it because I made him do that to me. Then he told me he was going to take me back to the group, to the other children.

"But not one tear," he said. "Not one complaint. Nothing, because God will get mad and the Devil will come and take your parents away. If that happens it will be your fault. Your fault." Then he told me, "Even if you try to tell anyone, they won't believe you. Who will believe you? They will believe me, the priest, the voice of God. You are a sinner. You are a woman." I was only eight years old.

This was the first time I was violated. I went back into the group as a totally different person. I was so confused I thought I would explode. I wanted to die from the shame and guilt I felt. I even wondered if it had been real, if it had happened to me. Did it happen to me? If it did, why didn't the other priest do something to save me?

I wanted to tell someone, to tell my grandmother who was there in the group. She came over to me as I walked in.

"What did you learn from him, Chinita?"

Chinita, little China girl, was my nickname. But I couldn't tell her anything so I didn't say a word.

Then, since the catechism class was over, we walked home. I didn't say a word. I felt like a spear was against my throat. I knew if I were to speak a word the spear would cut me all the way through and kill me.

This was the first time. But his abuse continued until I was sixteen years old.

My pain is the darkness where I have been. If I could show this grief, this pain inside, for people to see and understand, I would be in pieces. They would have to scrape me up and put me in a jar. And there would be Sonia, in pieces in the jar. All of us survivors have gone through this grieving experience. And still, to this day, only God knows how many others have gone through this experience and feel this pain. They feel alone.

The healing I have done for myself has recognized little Sonia's violation, pain, anger, and hatred for God and the Church. I have now reclaimed her as part of me and have allowed her to express herself by speaking my truth. Until this healing occurred, I wanted to bomb the church and kill priests. I fantasized about seeing mutilated priests dying in the street. Fortunately, I have evolved from that nightmare.

The most painful experience, if I was going to rank them, is feeling bereft of spirituality—the feeling that God hated me while being forced to go to church as a child, the constant message that God is love, and God loves children, and Jesus loves children while I was being violated by the representatives of this God. I was confused and hateful towards God—hateful toward seeing crosses in church and seeing people go into the church.

The abuse happened in many different places, but it was the same priest all the time. He had other priests with him in the rectory a couple of times with other girls. Since I was the youngest, these other priests made me watch them have sex with these other girls.

They were teenage girls, maybe fourteen or fifteen years old, and they looked like they were enjoying it. The girls would say, "Oh, Padre Carlitos, I like what you are doing." And he wanted me to watch that, because he wanted me to have the same attitude they had.

I remember one of the girl's name. She was Margarita. She would come and put her arms around him. They would start kissing and he would put his hand under her skirt. He would lay her down on this desk where there were books, pushing the books aside. She would lay right on top of the desk and he would enter her.

He would take off her blouse and her fancy brassiere. He would say to me, "I bought this for her because she is a good girl. She likes to come here and meet me every Wednesday. Maybe there is something you can learn from her."

Margarita was a beautiful teenager, just as I was a beautiful little girl. I hated it! I knew being beautiful and thin meant I was a target for men. I knew if I was beautiful, if I was thin, the same thing was going to happen to me as what I was witnessing happen to Margarita.

Padre Carlitos would have sex with Margarita with his Roman collar and his black robe on the entire time, . He pulled up the front of his robe and entered her vagina.

Padre Carlitos always wore his black robe when he had sex with the other girls, and he wore his black robe when he raped me. But now my mother has told me that he wears a white robe. I never saw him in a white robe and don't know if there is any significance to the change in colors.

Although I was forced to watch him have sex with this young girl, I didn't say a word. I didn't move, scream, or cry. Inside I was being torn apart, but no one knew. I realized that I could never be what he wanted me to be. I would only get more punishment for that.

When I was ten years old, I went to the church, this time to accompany my grandmother who wanted to pray and light a candle. Padre Carlitos came to her and spoke with her. When I saw him, my body froze and my mouth stopped salivating. I wanted to scream, I wanted to run, I wanted an earthquake, I wanted the church roof to fall. I wanted any catastrophe to happen so I would never have to see him again. Anything so he would not be able to touch me again.

But on this particular day, Padre Carlitos told my grandmother that my mother had approved confession for me with him. He needed to take me to the back of the rectory, because that is where God will be closer to me. The priest told my grandmother I would feel better giving my confession to him in private rather than in the confessional. Now I know this was a lie, but at the time I did not, and could not, question him or refuse to go with him.

I don't know how it happened. I don't remember what my grandmother said, because she was a woman who didn't trust people much. She knew who was good and who was not.

What I remember is that I was holding Padre Carlitos's hand and we were going to the back of the church, behind the altar. When we got behind the altar, he told me that I had been a bad little girl. He told me that I had been telling people about what he had been doing to me and that was not good. He told me I had broken a promise, to not tell anybody.

But I had not told anybody. I could not speak, I could not say anything. I was so afraid. I wanted to scream for my grandmother to come. I wanted somebody to surprise us there, behind the altar. I could hear the other kids playing outside, kicking a ball. I just couldn't understand what was happening. Here he was, reprimanding me for something I hadn't done. I was frozen with fear, not knowing what was happening or what was going to happen.

I couldn't run. My legs felt so heavy. Then he said he needed to go and prepare himself for my punishment. At that time he whistled, and an older man came from somewhere in the back of the church. He was a very old man, with a lot of facial wrinkles. He came over, but didn't look at me. He just pulled my panties down, and told me he needed to prepare me for initiation.

He took my panties off and put his fingers inside my vagina. Then he told me to walk. He wanted me to walk, with his fingers in my vagina. To walk from where we were to the other door where Padre Carlitos had disappeared through. Where Padre Carlitos would be waiting for me. So this older man had his two fingers inside my vagina and I had to walk like that. Almost like a squat position, and walk.

He was telling me how tight I was, and saying things like "You like this, don't you? You like this." And he said, "If you didn't like it, you would scream and run away. You like this. Padre Carlitos is right about you. You are sinful and mousy. What a shame. Your parents are such good people, and they had to have a daughter like you who likes to have sex with priests."

He told me this while I walked in that semi-squat position toward the direction of the confessional and the door that was to the side, leading into another room. I had to walk sideways. We walked through the door into the room where Padre Carlitos was waiting. He told the older man that it was OK for him to leave now. That man removed his fingers, his hand, away from my vagina.

"She is ready," the old man said. "She didn't kick. She didn't scream. She didn't do anything. She is ready." He left.

Padre Carlitos led me over to this desk, this table. He still had on his collar and his dress. I think of his robe, the garb of a priest, as a dress. To me he was a monster who wore a black dress. He lifted up his robe/dress and unzipped his pants.

"You know very well what this is," he told me. "And you like it. You have liked it so far. Now I am going to do to you the ultimate reason why you were born, and why God brought you to this earth. God made women to have sex, and children after that. Your sole purpose right here and now is to lay there. Open your legs, and let me bless you. And let me tell you, it is an honor for you to be in this position, because I am Padre Carlitos and I am God."

I started to sob, quietly. He put his big hand over my mouth and mounted me. I looked around, trying to find something I could look at and escape from the moment. I looked for a little hole in the ceiling or even a spider. Anything to distract me from what was happening. All I saw were books, big heavy books. They were foreign books that looked ancient, like they had never been read or even opened. I just looked at the books.

He begin to penetrate me and go inside of me. I burned, oh how I burned. I felt like it was a sword going through my soul.

And then it was over. When the pain got to be too much, I didn't feel anything. I didn't feel a thing. I promised myself that this wasn't happening. I pretended I was flying out of my body, and flying all over the room. I remember every little hole in the wall. The crucifix on the wall. I remember the tile on the floor and I remember the dust.

When he was done, he opened the drawer of that table and pulled out a clean pair of panties. He cleaned me with a towel and put the new panties on me. I thought I had peed on the table, but when I looked there was blood on the table, and this is what he was cleaning up. From me and the table. He gave me some lollipops. He gave me money so I could go buy whatever candy I wanted. He gave me five cents, which was a lot of money back then in El Salvador. You could buy a lot of candy with five cents.

Padre Carlitos knew I liked candy and knew what flavors were my favorites. He said he would give me more money and candy next time as the stupid people in the church gave him money all the time, because he was handsome and nice. Out of their contributions, he would give me money.

And then he said to me, "By the way, I was teasing you. You haven't talked to anyone about this. I was just testing you, to see if you had indeed talked to anyone, but since you didn't say anything to anyone that shows me you are a good girl. You listen well. This secret is between you, me, and God and it is your purpose in living. God creates women so they can procreate. It is in the Bible. God created men first, and, out of his rib, woman was born out of dust."

Then he brought me back to my grandmother, who was still praying. She was still kneeling, praying, and lighting candles. No one had heard me. My screams were inside myself, even though I thought that everyone could hear me. No one had heard a thing, and everything continued like it was normal. No catastrophe occurred except the violation of my body, spirit, and soul.

I knew I was the worst little girl who had ever lived. I didn't feel anything except physical and mental pain. I felt dirty and hated my body so much. I wished for the courage to cut myself up so he would never see me again. I never actually had that much courage, so I felt like a sick weakling—because I couldn't cut myself up into little pieces.

Carlitos punished me further by telling me that I was a pitiful little thing. His nickname for me was mousy. Ratoncito in Spanish. He picked that because he wanted me to believe that I was such a pathetic soul that even God didn't want me. He told me that even my own mother didn't want me. He told me those things and make me repeat them to him so I would learn and believe them.

Now, thinking about this abuse forty years later, I realized he was talking to himself when he called me mousy. If he had been talking to me, he should have called me Raton-cita, which is the feminine form of the noun in Spanish. By using the masculine form he was talking to himself.

This man, Carlos Villacorta, still has his own parish in San Miguel, El Salvador. I don't know if the other priest is still alive. There was another man involved who cleaned the church. That man was in cahoots with Carlos. I don't know if he is alive or not. And I don't care.

What is horrifying to me is that this man, Carlos, is still in a parish. And God knows what he is still doing to the children. My heart and my head tell me I am not the only one who has gone through this experience.

He destroyed my entire sense of self esteem. As a woman, I used to think that I was nothing but a thing, a sex toy for men, a mop. I was a couch, a something. I didn't believe I was someone special. Unfortunately, my relationships with men as an adult have been a mirror of what I experienced as a child. I didn't realize this until I was thirty-eight years old. That is when my whole world, as I knew it, changed.

I was a single parent, divorced, working like a mad dog to make ends meet. I decided to tell my parents about being abused while we were sitting in my doctor's office. I thought they would be there in support of me. In my pain, I thought they would at least be compassionate. but they were not. They asked me: "Why did you tell us in front of a stranger?" They were more concerned about their embarrassment than they were about my torment and grief.

To this day, they still do not support me. I think back to my experience as a little girl. I could not tell my parents about the abuse when it was happening so I was forced to endure the pain by myself. That day in the doctor's office was the same. Even though I told my parents, in the end I carried that pain alone there also. It broke my heart that my parents could not be there for me—that they thought my telling my story shamed me. They put more guilt on me for speaking out.

They told me things like, "It happened thirty years ago. Forgive and forget."

Although I turned forty-eight in June 2004, my memory of this abuse is still crystal clear. I hoped that, after all these years, it would be foggy or I would forget. But the memories are very clear.

I want people to understand that it is important to me, as I tell my story, that you see me as a grown woman. But you should remember that I was only a small child when I was abused. Please hold your judgments against me and avoid comments such as: "It happened a long time ago," or "You could have run," or "You could have kicked him." All of those judgments of guilt and shame do not help the survivor come to a place of understanding. Remember that I was eight years old when the violations started, and ten years old when I was first raped.

If you have children of your own or know other children who are ten years old, look at them. What do you think they would do if they had a man whom they considered to be like a god on top of them? What choices or options will they have?

When I turned sixteen, I became so enraged, so rebellious. I hated my mother. I really wanted to kill my mother, and, in my mind, I killed her many times. But, in actions, I couldn't. I decided that for the rest of my life I would never walk into a Catholic Church again.

Every time I would see Padre Carlitos, I would run the other way. I would rather have had my mother beat me to a pulp than ever be in the company of this man again. He would come to our house. He came to our house a couple of times during my teenage years. He wanted me to know, to really know, to be truly convinced, that my mother was in agreement with all that he had done to me. How did he prove this to me?

He told me that on a certain day he would come to my house, and I would see how my mother treated him. He said he would tell my mother all the things he had been doing with me. and my mother would be nice to him and hug him. That is exactly what happened.

I watched from my bedroom, the day I knew he was coming. I didn't tell anybody how I felt. I had so much shame and knew I couldn't hide anywhere.

I believed there was this eye of God that watched every-thing and everyone. I knew there was this physical eye of God that watched me wherever I went. I never had any peace, even when I tried to hide. How could I hide from the eye of God?

On this particular day I saw him as he sat and talked with my mother. She brought him lemonade. She was so attentive to him. She asked him, "What can I do for you? Please come over here." I heard her tell him how much she liked the work he was doing in the church—and how cute he was. She told him, "Because you are so young, people trust you more."

I peed in my pants. I watched all of this from the window in my bedroom. At that moment, in my mind, I believed my mother knew about the abuse I had gone through. I believed my mother had given her permission for him to sexually abuse me. This caused me to be estranged from my mother, and it has taken a lot of work on my part to develop a trusting relationship with her.

I have not been back to El Salvador since I entered the United States in December of 1976 as a married woman. I have considered returning to El Salvador these last two years (2002–2004), knowing that I am now a strong woman and no longer that broken little girl. But when it gets near the time to go, to actually buy the tickets, I am not ready. When Hell freezes over, maybe I will consider it, but probably not even then. Just remembering my childhood brings me so much fear, but it is the fear of a child.

The few times when Padre Carlitos told me he would come to my house and prove what he told me about my mother giving me to him, he actually came to my house and talked with my mother. This was enough to prove to me, as a child, that he was telling me the truth. I was convinced.

Now I don't see myself going to El Salvador. And this hurts me. It is my country, and I would like to get to know it. I want to feel safe, no matter where I go or where I am. A part of me knows that and acknowledges that fact. But I still don't think I will return.

People have a different perception of priests in countries like mine. Even nowadays, sexual abuse by priests is not talked about or discussed in the papers. I don't believe people in El Salvador would hear my story and tell me they were sorry for poor little Sonia. They won't take a stand against this sexual abuse by the priests.

I read in the newspaper last year that the bishops in El Salvador receive cases of priests abusing children every year, and they burn the case reports—year after year— it is just paper to them. There is no sense of accountability to them. They are still living back in the stone ages where people just go to church and give both the priest and the Church money. Priests are considered gods. People go about their merry way and never question what the priests are doing. In the eyes of many, the priests can do no wrong.

So I don't think there is even a platform there for people to hear my story. And my family doesn't talk about it. They still see this priest, Father Carlitos, today. The abuse he inflicted on me has never been an issue for my family to deal with. They have never been outraged against the Church because of what happened to me. It is like it is Sonia's story, and my family is detached from that.

I still have family in El Salvador. To my knowledge, nothing has been done about any of the priests who abuse children. Priests abusing children is considered permissible. It is allowed. And it is condoned. And it is a crime.

And I am here to tell you all that clergy sexual abuse is one of the most hideous crimes in the whole wide world and cannot continue to be tolerated by the Catholic Church.

I was a victim of this hideous crime, but survived to tell you about it. This is due in great part to the ten years of psychotherapy I spent with Dr. Gloria Denkins, Ph.D., and my healing using the vibrations of Flower Essence.

I am now a survivor and a thriver. One of the reasons I am in this world is to tell you the truth that you have just read and make sure no other child suffers alone in shame and guilt at the hands of clergy. It is fitting that we ask every Christian clergy a simple question. "What would Jesus have done?"

Terry's Story

Editor's Comments

Terry's story of being sexually abused by a Catholic priest is unique in many ways, but it also shares some commonality with the stories of clergy sexual abuse by other survivors.

One common trait in the priests who were abusing children was their complete disregard and disdain for secular legal authority. The priests, and especially the bishops, considered the sexual abuse of children to be a sin, to be dealt with according to the laws of the Church and not a crime to be dealt with according to the criminal laws of the United States.

In all cases, the Church, through the bishops, was more concerned with the reputation and financial well being of the Church than with the well being of the victims. The misplaced concerns of the Church have been shown in many ways. In Terry's case, he waited ten years before reporting the abuse to the San Francisco Archdiocese. After telling Terry that this was the first indication the San Francisco

Archdiocese had that Keegan was molesting children, a statement totally at odds with the facts, the Monsignor promised Terry he would inform the Archbishop of the abuse.

Then he said to Terry, "But you know that Father Keegan is a fine priest and I am sure you don't want to bring any embarrassment upon the Church."

Even today, twenty five years after Terry reported the abuse, it is difficult to understand how a monsignor in the Catholic Church could characterize a priest who had sodomized a ten year old boy as "a fine priest." Perhaps the Catholic Church should be asked if a priest sodomizing ten year old boys is considered a fine priest.

One other factor stands out in Terry's story. He was the son of a California state senator, a man who would have been elected mayor of San Francisco. Keegan had no fear of sexually abusing this boy, in spite of the political connections of his family.

The concept that sexual abuse of children is a sin, and not a crime, and that bishops deal with sins and not crimes was emphasized in June 2004 by a statement made at the Dallas Bishops Conference by Salesian Cardinal Oscar Rodriguez of Honduras, who has been mentioned as a leading candidate to succeed Pope John Paul II.

The statement was in regard to reports that the Salesian order had transferred priests from country to country even after the priests had been accused of sexually molesting and abusing children. This assisted the priests in avoiding law enforcement efforts to arrest them, and allowed the Church to avoid messy

*and expensive lawsuits such as have been filed in the
United States in the recent past.*

*Cardinal Oscar Rodriguez was quoted as stat-
ing, "For me it would be a tragedy to reduce the role of
a pastor to that of a cop. I'd be prepared to go to jail
rather than harm one of my priests."*

*This statement, taken at face value, seems to
mean the cardinal would rather protect his priests
than the children in his care. This principle, sadly, is
born out in every survivor story in this book.*

My father would have been elected mayor of
San Francisco in November, 1967. He was a
successful California state senator and the
Democratic front runner in heavily Democratic San
Francisco. As an Irish Catholic, he had support from
the many Irish Catholics who made up a significant
percentage of voters in San Francisco.

My father had another advantage; the support of Father
Peter Keegan, a Catholic priest at Saint Cecilia's Parish. Father Keegan, a native San Franciscan, was a
strong and effective political supporter for my father.
He came from a well known Italian-American family
that had been active in the San Francisco longshore-
men operations for years. He gathered support from
the Italian-American community, which was a major
factor in San Francisco politics. My father's campaign

manager, Joe Alioto, was a prominent San Franciscan in his own right and also an Italian-American.

Unfortunately my father never lived to be elected mayor. He died on the handball court on May 26, 1967. He was fifty-one years old, leaving behind my mother, Frances, and my two older brothers, Tom and Tim, who were both students at UCLA. Then there was me, ten years old, and Father Peter Keegan, the Catholic priest who molested and raped me. Let me explain how Peter Keegan played such an important role in the life of our family.

Peter Keegan entered into the life of the Eugene McAteer family in 1962, fresh out of Saint Patrick's Seminary in Menlo Park, California. His first assignment as a young priest was to St. Cecilia's Parish in the Sunset District. He worked under the direction of Monsignor Harold Collins, who at the time was professing that St. Cecilia's was the finest, greatest, and best parish in San Francisco.

St. Cecilia's was the home parish to many of the major political families in San Francisco. In addition to our family, Leo McCarthy and his family lived in St. Cecilia's. Leo was the Democratic majority leader in the California State Assembly and later Lt. Governor of California. Terry Francois, an important San Francisco politician, lived in St. Cecilia's. If you were to examine the records of the time, you would probably find that almost half of the San Francisco politicians lived in St. Cecilia's parish.

In some ways, it was an odd relationship, my father being such great friends with a Catholic priest. In other ways, it was perfect because my father's family was not Catholic. My father really didn't have a faith. He grew up in an orphanage because his father, my grandfather, left him when he was very young and his mother, my grandmother, had a nervous breakdown. My father was placed in St. Vincent's Orphanage for several years, until eventually his mother recovered. At that time, he went to live with her in the Mission District of San Francisco, attending Mission High School, class of 1934, and later the University of California, Berkeley, class of 1938.

Although my mother was a devout born and raised Irish Catholic, when she met my father he didn't profess any faith. My father was intelligent enough to realize that being a Catholic in San Francisco was politically expedient. Even then he had political aspirations and wanted to go into politics and lead "The City," as San Francisco was known. Since my mother was Catholic, my father chose to be baptized Catholic by Monsignor Collins at St. Cecilia's in the early 1950's.

In 1962, Father Peter Keegan, fresh out of the seminary, arrived at St. Cecilia's. He had grown up on Dolores Street and knew San Francisco well. He recognized that being assigned to St. Cecilia's was his opportunity to become someone powerful. He latched on to the various political families in St. Cecilia's, but became especially close to the McAteer family.

By 1963, Peter Keegan was an integral part of our family life. And it was great. Peter Keegan was fun to be around. He was the kind of Catholic priest my father wanted to know and socialize with. Actually, Peter Keegan was the ideal priest for a politician. He would tell my father, "Hey, don't worry. You know the rules can be bent. I am your friend." Or he would say, "Don't call me Father Keegan, just call me Pete." Nobody addressed him as Father Keegan. We just said, "Hi, Pete."

Our life, both in politics and in St. Cecilia's Parish, was good. My father, originally elected to the California State Senate in 1958, was reelected in 1964 and again in 1966. In 1967, he announced that he was running for mayor of San Francisco. Peter Keegan was right beside him. My father was going to do well in the Catholic community because of Peter Keegan being a Roman Catholic priest and he was going to do well in the Italian-American community because of Peter Keegan's Italian connections. Of course the Irish-American community was in our corner because both my mother and father were Irish-Americans. At that time, those two ethnic communities were the biggest voting blocs in San Francisco.

By this time, Peter Keegan was almost a member of our immediate family. He celebrated Thanksgiving and Christmas with us. Although he didn't have a key to our front door, if he had asked, he would have been given one. He was part of our family.

People loved him because he was a social animal, the kind of man who was the life of the party. He loved cocktail parties, and people in general loved to have him at their parties. People just enjoyed being around Peter Keegan.

Then my father died on the handball court, right in the middle of his campaign for mayor. His death was, of course, a major event in San Francisco political circles, as he was the favorite to win the election. All of a sudden, he was dead. His successor had to be picked, but first, of course, was his funeral.

The funeral was impressive to a young boy of ten. It seemed the entire Roman Catholic community of San Francisco was there at the funeral mass held in St. Cecilia's. All the top San Francisco and California Democratic political figures were there. Of course the top Catholic leaders were there also. But the funeral mass was said by Father Peter Keegan, not Monsignor Collins.

Less than a week after the funeral, a big black limousine pulled up in front of our house on Santa Ana Avenue. My mother and I were the only two people in the house because my brothers had returned to school. This visitor was my dad's campaign manager, Joe Alioto. Joe told us that he would run for mayor only if my mother endorsed and supported him. My mother agreed, and the rest is history. Joe easily won the election in November, just as my father would have if he had not died on the handball court.

Between my father's death in May and the election in November, life went on. My mother was a well known political figure, as she had been the wife of a California State Senator and was friends with all of the Democratic leaders and workers in the State, especially in San Francisco.

I was not aware of any discussions that took place between my mother and the campaign manager for Joe Alioto, but I am sure they asked her to attend numerous political and social functions in support of Joe's bid for mayor. Of course, she needed an escort for these functions. Who would be a better escort for a recently widowed Catholic woman than a Catholic priest? Father Peter Keegan stepped in and fulfilled the role of escort whenever the occasion called for my mother's presence.

Peter Keegan must have enjoyed his role as an escort for my mother, for he continued to be her safe, non-threatening escort for several years. My mother, young at fifty, was a bright energetic woman, but she had no desire to date anyone. Keegan was a safe option that provided an opportunistic solution for both. It gave my mother a safe, fun-to-be-with escort and Keegan an entrance into the top level social and political functions that he so craved.

Keegan stayed involved in the affairs of the McAteer family. When my brother Tom married his wife Dana in Los Angeles in November of 1967, Father Keegan said the mass for them. For the next nine years, Keegan continued to be in our life. He played golf with my mom. He saw my mother socially. Every year I would get a Christmas present from Peter Keegan. I was always cool to him, but not openly enough that my mother would ask, "Gee, Terry, why aren't you nice to Father Keegan?"

It was not that I wasn't nice. I just kept my distance. When he came in, I would go to another room. When he said, "Hi" I would say "Hi, Father. Nice to see you. How are you?" We were always cordial, but I never wanted to be around him again. Not after Disneyland.

My story takes place in the summer of 1967, shortly after the death of my father. Keegan came to our house and told my mother:

"Frances, you have had a rough summer and it would be good for you to have a few days to yourself. Terry has also had a lousy summer and deserves to have some fun. Therefore I would like to take him to Disneyland for the weekend. Would that be OK with you?"

My mother thought that was a fabulous idea. Father Keegan was sympathetic to her and willing to take me to Disneyland. I don't know who paid for the trip and I am not even sure what month it was. Those details are unimportant to a ten year old boy, excited about going to Disneyland with such a fun companion as Father Keegan. The morning of our trip, Keegan picked me up at our home. Two other boys were already in the car when I got in.

Father Keegan, the two other boys who were about thirteen years old, and I flew to Orange County and stayed at the Disneyland Hotel. I remember the room well. It was not in the high rise portion. There were a lot of single story rooms around the Disneyland Hotel at that time. We stayed in two of them, arriving early in the afternoon and we checked right in. The two older boys stayed in one room, while Father Keegan and I stayed in the other. Both rooms had twin beds, so it seemed like a natural way to divide up the rooms among the four of us.

We went to the swimming pool that afternoon and had a good old time thinking about getting up early the next day to go to Disneyland. The afternoon went on into the evening and Father Keegan was such a character. He really was a fun person to be around. He would let anything go. You could say "damn" or "Hell" and he would say it right back to you, making all of us laugh. At those times, we never thought of him as a priest. He didn't wear his Roman collar on the Disneyland trip, just an open shirt. He was always a lot of fun to be with.

After dinner we went to bed. The next morning I was awakened about 5:00 AM. It was still dark outside and Father Keegan was crawling into bed with me. I was half awake and half asleep and wondering what was going on.

Keegan started fondling my genitals. I was really scared as this was definitely not enjoyable. Nobody had ever put their hands down my shorts and touched my testicles before—not my mother nor my father. My mom had always called them "Your privates." Suddenly Father Keegan had his hands on "my privates" as he fondled me. I was only ten years old and not well developed in the genital area. Father Keegan was using his saliva to masturbate himself.

He then turned my body around in the bed. Now understand he weighed about 220 or 230 pounds and was about six feet tall. I was ten years old and small for my age. I didn't know what was going on, but I didn't like it.

After turning my body around, he proceeded to turn my head toward the bottom of the bed and put his genitals into my face. And I thought, "Oh my God!" I had never seen anybody's genitals like that. My father was a modest person and my brothers were modest. You just didn't walk around our house naked. It wasn't acceptable behavior.

Now this man's genitals were shoved in my face. I remember the heat and sweat dripping from him as he became excited.

He gained superiority over me by using his weight on top of my head and chest. He would lean his body on my chest or my head and suffocate me. I gasped for air, trying desperately to breathe. That was how he forced me into submission. Then he put his penis into my mouth and ejaculated.

I had never experienced anything like this before. It was really bizarre. I spit the sperm out, gasping for air. At that point, Father Keegan spun me around and cuddled me. We were sort of in a fetal position, with him behind me. He told me, "Everything is fine, Terry. This is no big deal. Father Keegan loves you. You love Father Keegan, don't you?"

I replied, "Yes."

"Well, thank you, because Father Keegan thought you did and you have just shown Father Keegan how much you love him." Boy, this was a strange way to show love, but I was so young I was unable to comprehend what had just occurred. And I was also scared and therefore said nothing.

His cuddling me went on. It was an hour-long process. It was pitch dark when he started and then there was daylight coming into the bedroom by the time it ended.

I finally said, "I have to go to the bathroom, Father." So he let me get out of the bed and I went into the bathroom, took a shower, and cleaned up. I was ready to go to Disneyland for the day.

At that point, he got the other two boys next door and we went to Disneyland. He was on me like a hawk. The other two boys were off doing their thing. I never knew them before and I never saw them after.

He let us go all through Disneyland, running around, having fun. Those two boys would go anywhere they wanted to go, but he was with me on each and every ride. Whatever ride I went on, he went with me. Now I see that this was his means of not allowing me to associate with the other two kids and potentially saying something like "This weird thing happened to me last night." Father Keegan wanted to make sure he stayed in charge of the situation.

So we spent the day at Disneyland. For a kid, it was a great way to take your mind off any problems, just having a great day at Disneyland, getting to go on all the rides you wanted. Disneyland in those days didn't stay open late like it does now. I think they closed at five or six, and you would go home. When we got back to the Disneyland Hotel, I don't remember if we went to the pool or not. I do remember having dinner.

I remember going to bed that night in my white pajamas. I had these white pajamas with a draw string in the pants. They were very nice pajamas.

I went to bed that night not thinking about anything, just totally exhausted after a long day at Disneyland. Again, at five o'clock in the morning, Father Keegan was back. The first time Father Keegan was somewhat aggressive, but also passive, in this caring nature. The second morning he was aggressive, and animalistic. He was determined to dominate the situation, which of course was evident because he outweighed me by 150 pounds or so.

If I had known then what I know today, I would have gotten up and knocked on the boys' door in the next room. But remember, this was Father Keegan! For half my life he had been a close friend of my family. How could he do anything bad? This must be OK. All those thoughts raced through my mind. And remember I was just a ten-year-old child.

Keegan at that point proceeded to try and do the same thing as he had done the first morning. However I fought back this time, as I did not want to have his penis in my mouth again. He again used his weight to gain leverage on me, mainly by suffocation. But this time it was not working. He did succeed in getting my head down against his genitals, but I wouldn't open my mouth. It was a pretty bad scene we were in.

I kept saying "No, Father. No, Father."

Keegan finally realized this was not going to work for him. So he turned me around again and attempted to take off my pajamas. He got the pajama bottoms off by undoing the draw string. The pants ballooned out and he pulled them off. Then he wanted to take off my shirt.

In the process of his aggression, my pajama top ripped because he couldn't get the buttons undone. Finally the shirt came off. I was naked.

Then he now got on top of me as I laid flat on the bed and used the pillow and his weight once again to gain control over me, placing the pillow over my head to silence me. The weight of his body on top of me was too much for me to resist. Then he laid on top of me and used his saliva to masturbate himself.

He used his legs to separate my legs and attempted to sodomize me. I am now an adult and this is still the worst pain I have ever experienced. His erect adult penis was forced into a small child's anus. It was so painful I screamed while he struggled to get his penis into me. I don't know if he ejaculated inside of me or outside of me. But I had another problem.

Father Keegan had ruptured a number of blood vessels in my anus. It was so painful and I was mortified because of the excruciating pain. I was physically hurt really bad by this priest.

He finished his act and laid there again in his cuddling state. It was now getting light so we were able to see. I laid there in pain as he kept telling me again and again, "Hey, Terry, thank you. Everything is fine. Father Keegan loves you, and you love Father Keegan."

At that point I said, "I would like to get into the shower please."

He kept his arm around me. Why? I couldn't run away and escape. I was in Los Angeles, a literal captive at this point at the Disneyland Hotel.

Finally, he let me get up as the sunlight came pouring into the room. As I got up, I looked back at the bed where there was a sizable amount of blood on the sheets. In retrospect, it was blood mixed with semen and sweat, but, at that young age, a little blood is enough to make you think you are going to die. It probably was only a minuscule amount, but there it was, spread around on the sheets, and my rear was killing me.

I cried "Oh, my God!" and ran into the bathroom and locked the door. I was mortified. What was I going to tell my mother? What could I tell my mother? I sat with my back against the bathroom door crying. I just wanted to go home. How could I get home?

Eventually, with the door locked, and Keegan talking on the other side saying, "Come on, Terence. We have to go to Disneyland. I know you want to go to Disneyland. We will have a fun day in Disneyland. Get in the shower and let's get going," Finally I gave in.

I got into the shower. The bleeding had stopped at that point. I pulled myself together and got some clothes on. I asked him to put some clothes by the door because I didn't want to show him any part of my body again. By the end of my shower, he had gone next door and awakened the two other boys. They were getting ready.

Nothing more was said by Father Keegan. We actually had a great day in Disneyland. Then we flew home. We got in his car and he drove the other two boys home first. And then on the way to my house I got his indoctrination.

"Now remember, you are not going to say anything to your mother about this. This is just between you and me. This is something that we need between us. Father Keegan loves you and you love Father Keegan"—all that kind of horse shit.

I didn't know it at the time, but Keegan had been transferred from St. Cecilia's to Epiphany shortly before he took me to Disneyland. After Epiphany, he was transferred to St. Vincent de Paul and then to Mary's Help Hospital. All of those transfers were intended to keep him away from kids. It is now apparent to me that the Catholic Church was aware of what Keegan was doing. Unfortunately, the transfers, intended to stop his sexual abuse of children, didn't work.

When complaints continued about Keegan molesting kids, the Archdiocese of San Francisco transferred him to the Diocese of Santa Rosa. He was assigned to two different parishes in Santa Rosa before so many accusations were lodged that the Santa Rosa bishop was forced to yank his collar. Keegan fled to Mexico.

When we reached my home, Keegan came in the house and talked with my mom. He probably had a cocktail with her as I went up to my room and unpacked.

The next morning, my mother asked me as she was going through the laundry.

"How did your pajamas get ripped?"

I know I turned a bright red in sheer fright. I am not sure if she saw me.

"Oh, mom, I was wrestling with the other two boys and somehow my PJs got ripped." I had to think fast, because I wasn't going to tell my mother I had been sexually abused. Besides, at ten years of age, how do you tell your mother that the priest who buried your father and who has been in your house for all these years has sodomized you? Of course, at that time I had never heard the word sodomize. I mean, I had never ever talked with my mother about my penis. We had never discussed anything close to what I had just experienced at the Disneyland Hotel. I simply didn't have the vocabulary or the emotional maturity to discuss what had happened.

That was the last of it for nine years. I never said anything to anyone except my friend, Greg Cronin, who was thirteen or fourteen. I knew him through the neighborhood. He told me Father Keegan had invited him up to Tahoe for the weekend and how great it would be and how he was looking forward to it.

I turned to him and said, "Greg, I want you to know something. Get out of this. Do not go. I was molested by Peter Keegan down at Disneyland. I don't want the same thing to happen to you. That is why he is taking you to Tahoe." Fortunately Greg heeded my advice and didn't go.

That was the only time I mentioned the molestation until I was nineteen years old and went to the church to tell them about Keegan's abuse of me. I decided I needed to do something about Keegan, but did not want to involve my mother, because she wouldn't be able to handle it.

I phoned a good friend of mine from high school, Father Vincent Ring, a pastor in San Bruno—a really good guy and a great history teacher.

I phoned him and said, "I need your help to see someone in the diocese so I can tell them what happened to me because I am worried that other kids have also been molested by Peter Keegan." Father Ring agreed to help me.

It was the fall of 1977, and I was twenty years old, not nineteen. Father Ring arranged an appointment for me with the number two guy in the archdiocese. I was introduced to a monsignor who listened to me. I told him my story and said, "I want you to take some action against Peter Keegan."

He commiserated with me. "It was a long time ago. You are the first complaint we have ever heard about Peter Keegan. I am sorry it happened to you, but he is up in Santa Rosa now. We don't have any jurisdiction over him. That is Bishop Hurley's area in Santa Rosa."

I replied, "I would like to speak with Archbishop Quinn."

He indicated to me that he would take my case to the archbishop, and that he would keep me advised. Then he said, "But, you know that Father Keegan is a fine priest. I am sure you don't want to bring any embarrassment upon the Church. We will look into this and get back to you."

I knew I was being patronized up one side and down the other. When I left his office I got into the elevator on the third floor and burst into tears.

Father Ring had been nice enough to wait outside for me. When I got into his car, he could see I had been crying. I had lost. They weren't going to do anything about Father Keegan molesting little kids. Later I received a letter from the Archdiocese of San Francisco stating, "Thank you, and wishing you the best." I still have this correspondence, which is rather damning for the Church. Because I am one of the few people who not only told the Church early on about Keegan but I also have a record of my correspondence which shows that in 1977, I went to the highest authorities available and told them Father Peter Keegan is a pedophile with a long history of molesting boys. Subsequent to this I became aware that scores of boys were molested after I told the Archdiocese of San Francisco in 1977 what Keegan had done to me.

Obviously I had lost with the San Francisco Archdiocese, so I wrote to Bishop Hurley in the Santa Rosa diocese, telling him what had happened and that I hoped he would take action against Peter Keegan. I received another patronizing letter, this time from Bishop Hurley. It read something like: "Thank you very much. We are keeping an eye on Father Keegan, keeping him away from contact with young children."

Well, the reality is that he stayed in contact with young children. Nobody did anything. The other thing I found out later is that a number of complaints had been filed about Peter Keegan prior to 1977 when I told the two dioceses. Keegan had been moved from St. Vincent de Paul to Mary's Help Hospital solely because of a San Francisco police report.

After the Disneyland trip, Peter stayed in touch with my family. He said the mass when one of my brothers was married. He continued to play golf with my mother and escort her to various social and political functions. This changed in 1977 after I went to the archdiocese.

In 1977, after telling the San Francisco Archdiocese, I knew I had to tell my mother. By then, I was twenty years old. I told her I had something important to tell her.

"You remember that time Keegan took me to Disney-land? Well, he molested me."

That was basically all I said to her. But that was enough for her to understand how tragic it had been. After that, she told Keegan I had told her about the trip to Disney-land, and from then on the relationship slowly ended.

Most mothers probably would have gone out with a hatchet and tried to castrate him. But the molestation had happened ten years before and she is not that kind of person, she is not vindictive, She is a good mom, who came out of a Victorian world, where you see no evil, speak no evil, and hear no evil. That was her world.

We have now traveled in time from 1967 when I went to Disneyland, to 1977 when I told the Diocese, and since then my life continued. I got married, earned a Ph.D. in education from the University of San Francisco, and had two children.

In 1994, I was running for the office of superintendent of education in Nevada County. I was having a real tough race, my first attempt at any elected office.

One day in the middle of the afternoon, I came home early. I had been at work as assistant superintendent of schools and came home because I had campaign work to do and get ready for a long night of campaign events. I walked through the front door, and my wife Liz greeted me and said:

"Terry, you better sit down."

"OK, what happened now?" I replied.

"Did you read today's Chronicle?"

"No, I haven't had time."

"You need to read the lead story." she said, and handed me the paper.

The lead story was about three boys in Santa Rosa who had filed suit against a number of priests. One of the priests was Peter Keegan. The Santa Rosa Diocese said "We had no prior knowledge of this." The Archdiocese of San Francisco was quoted as saying, "We had no prior knowledge of this. We have never had any accusations against Peter Keegan."

I finished reading the article and looked up at my wife. I said, "They are lying!"

She said "I knew you would say that."

"I need to talk to that reporter about that quote. Is that exactly what they said?"

My wife replied, "I have already phoned the reporter, Don Lattin, of the San Francisco Chronicle."

"What did he say?" I asked.

"Well, he said the archdiocesan spokesperson said, 'Nope, we have no knowledge of prior problems with Father Keegan.'"

That floored me. Quinn was still the archbishop of San Francisco. I had told his assistant, the monsignor I spoke with in late 1977, seventeen years before, and Quinn should have known. The monsignor had clearly stated to me that he would be taking this matter to Archbishop Quinn.

I picked up the phone and called Don Lattin, the San Francisco Chronicle reporter. This was two weeks before the elections in Nevada County, which is about 120 miles or so east of San Francisco. People from the Bay Area drive through Nevada County on their way to and from Reno and Tahoe.

I said, "Don, this is Terry McAteer, Senator Gene McAteer's son. The Church is not telling the truth. And that is not OK." I told him the story of what had happened to me in Disneyland with Father Keegan. Lattin said "I will phone you back in a few minutes."

"I will tell you what, Don. You can run the story with two caveats. One is you can't write about where I live or what my job is. I don't want this to become a major factor in this election up here. Second of all, I need you to read me the story before it goes to press."

Don replied, "I have to do my homework. See if you are who you say you are."

I said, "That is fine."

Then Don wanted some details. He asked me about my dad's funeral and other personal items. He phoned back in an hour.

"You are who you say you are."

And I replied, "Of course I am who I say I am." In my mind I was thinking that this is not something I would want to lie about.

Don said, "This is a monumental story. I will phone you back in another couple of hours after I have done some source checking and written the story."

A couple of hours later, he phones me back and read me the story. I told him "It is fine. You can run it."

With that, the lead article in the next day's San Francisco Chronicle was that a former state senator's son was molested by a San Francisco priest.

My mother read the article and was beside herself. When I talked with her, she just said, "Oh my God!" My brothers were outraged, saying "Oh, my God. Why did you have to go public?" and a lot of other things. But the answer was quite simple. The answer to all of their questions was truth. I have been lied to by the Catholic Church and by Father Keegan and I believe that, when you tell the truth, the right thing will happen.

I received scores of letters and phone calls. It somehow stayed out of the media here in Nevada County, which was fine. Unless you took the San Francisco Chronicle or watched the evening news on TV, you would not know about it. Everyone phoned, from Oprah Winfrey to channels 2, 4, 5, and 7 in the Bay Area. They all wanted a piece of the story. I wasn't ready to give them what they wanted, mainly because I still had a campaign to manage and an election to win.

Two weeks later, I won the election, which was great. During this two weeks, my mother's house was inundated with phone calls from friends and letters from people I hadn't seen in years. I received upwards of 250 letters, which was nice. A lot of my close friends phoned me up here in Nevada County and were aghast. They never knew anything like this had ever happened, because it was just not something you made public.

The trial with the three boys moved on. The lawyers wanted to hear my story. They wanted to subpoena me and so forth. In the process, the Archdiocese of San Francisco phoned me and said, "We would like to settle with you."

Well, that was pretty amazing. I told them "You can talk with my attorney."

I have a close lawyer friend in San Francisco, Pam Sayad. I told the archdiocese to deal with her. A lawsuit was filed. One of my issues was I thought the statue of limitations would have run out.

The Church set up a meeting with my attorney and settled my claim. I can't disclose the amount of the settlement just by the terms of the settlement, but the Church did settle with me. Part of the settlement was to keep me shut up and out of the way which was fine with me. Actually it was not just the money thing. I have a great job, and a fabulous family, and, at this point in time, we are doing very well. My two children, who are eleven and thirteen, have no knowledge of this, which is just fine. I don't want to sit them down and talk to them about a priest hurting their father. We go to mass every Sunday as a family. When they are adults, we as a family can sit down and discuss this matter. But for right now, for an eleven and thirteen year old, it is just not the right time. My wife and I have agreed to protect our kids from that.

I thought that was the end of the road, but the story continued. The scandal in Boston raised its ugly head in that it was all over the papers about many pedophile priests and their victims. These last six months (April to October, 2002) have been very painful and difficult for me, mainly because I have read many of the stories of kids molested by these pedophile priests. Many of them are similar to my story: manipulation by the priests and bishops, the Church closing its eyes to the reality of the problem, the transfer of abusive priests to other parishes, etc. It has been a tough six months on me. Probably a tougher six months than any other time I have ever experienced.

One thing I can tell you I have learned is that the older the kids are, the more damaging it is psychologically to them. I would say the psychological damage to me was not as great as it was to other kids, mainly because I was only ten years old. I had not experienced my own sexuality. Sexuality was not something I knew. My trust was betrayed by Peter Keegan, but my sexuality wasn't betrayed because I didn't know myself as a sexual being at that point.

I see many more problems in young teenage boys who suffered severe psychological ramifications as a result of the sexual abuse—questioning their own sexuality. Are they gay? Can they make commitments? All these kinds of dynamics take place. I can tell you it wasn't monumental to me in terms of who I was as a human being.

As the story broke six or eight months ago, around March or April of 2002, I read in the San Francisco Chronicle that District Attorney Hallinan had subpoenaed all the personnel files of the Archdiocese of San Francisco. I have a friend, Andy Clark, who is an assistant DA. I wrote a note to Andy that basically asked him to watch out for my interests. It said:

"Obviously, some day I would love to get Peter Keegan. But, until the law changes, which will allow that to happen, I want you to protect my interest because you are going to get all those files. My correspondence to the Church is going to be in them, and I would appreciate that as a friend." Andy phoned me and said:

"Terry, thanks so much for the note. We are getting Keegan's file and Elliott Beckelman will be handling the case."

"What do you mean, the case?" I asked Andy.

And he said, "Well, Keegan is one of the ones high on our list because we have knowledge of other kids being molested by Keegan."

"Oh really?" I said.

"Yeah" he replied. "I don't know how many at this point, but there is a number."

"Wow!" I said. "What are you going to do about it?"

"The law changed in California. The law allows you, within a year of notification, to file criminal charges."

I was quite taken aback by that. "Do you mean you can still get him?"

"Yeah" Andy said, "because the California statutes have changed." At that point I got to thinking about it.

Elliott Beckelman phoned me a couple of days later. He is an assistant DA, assigned to these cases. He told me that he had Keegan's file, and that they believed the number is somewhere in the neighborhood of eighty other kids in San Francisco and the North Bay who have been molested by Keegan. He was their "Number One Animal."

When he told me this, my only reaction was to gasp, "Oh, my God."

Then Elliott said to me, "And you, Terry, happen to be our number one witness because you are not coming forward now for the first time and telling us this. You told the Church in 1977 what was happening. Everything that has happened after 1977 is in the Church's knowledge base."

It has been an interesting ride since then. We will have to watch and see if they can capture Keegan. There is a warrant out for his arrest. I don't know exactly where they are on that. They have hauled in some of the other guys, but Keegan is out of country or running around as a fugitive. We will see what happens to him. If he does go to trial, I will be a witness relative to his case. Maybe we will have some justice, final justice after thirty-five years.

Postscript

Peter Keegan was arrested by the FBI in Mexico on March 2, 2003. After being held for some months, he was released due to legal technicalities. His present whereabouts are unknown. It is known that, during his time in Mexico, the Archdiocese of San Francisco continued to pay him his monthly pension check. It was also reported that the San Francisco Archdiocese paid out in excess of $2.4 million for Keegan's legal costs, settlements with victims, medical treatments, and therapy costs.

Jennifer's Story

Editor's Comments

Jennifer's abuse illustrates a common theme among the survivors. The priests had access to the children with the full knowledge and permission of the parents. Of the eight survivors telling their stories in this book, only Mary's parents were unaware that she was spending time alone with a Catholic priest. The rest all spent time with the priests with the full knowledge and approval of their parents.

Jennifer was taken on week-long trips by her abusive priest with the approval of her parents. She visited Monsignor Francis's apartment with the knowledge of her mother. Terry was taken to Disneyland with the full knowledge and consent of his mother. Mike, Steve, and Luke's parents were thrilled that their sons were receiving so much attention from a Catholic priest. Sonia was walked to the church by her grandmother, and turned over to the abusing priest. Sharan's parents knew she was being driven home by Father Ortino and they had no reason to disapprove or be concerned.

It should also be pointed out that Terry was the first survivor in this book to report his abuse, and that was ten years after it happened. Children were simply not able to report the abuse they were suffering at the time they were being abused.

I started first grade at Saint Bede's grammar school in Hayward, California, in the fall of 1978. My father was the grand knight of the Hayward Knights of Columbus, Council 1615, which included both Saint Bede's and All Saints parishes. My parents moved to Union City, just over the Hayward city limit, in 1971, the year before I was born. They continued to belong to Saint Bede's because they were so active in the parish.

Monsignor George J. Francis was the priest and pastor of Saint Bede's then and had been for many years. He was responsible for having raised a great deal of money, which had been used to build a huge church. All the people in the parish worshipped him. He thought he was a king.

Monsignor Francis was the man who raped me when I was seven years old and continued to abuse me for years. I found out later that I was not the first seven-year-old girl he had raped and abused and I was not the last. I was one in a series of young girls that he groomed and abused. After a few years of abusing one girl, he moved on to another seven year old girl. I have since found out that he was abusing more than one girl at a time.

My mom says he charmed us. He had us and the whole parish believing he was the best thing that had ever happened to Saint Bede's.

Monsignor Francis walked around in the school yard during lunchtime. All the little kids, especially the girls, would flock around him. The famous quote in Saint Bede's was, "Look how Monsignor loves the children, just like Jesus loved the little children."

My mother says he started charming us, as a family, long before I entered the first grade. One of the things he did was to select me as the queen for the Spring Carnival. This was a big event in the school year, and an honor for both the queen and her family. Mother saved a picture of me, as the queen, with two other little girls who acted as "my court."

Years later, I was to discover that Monsignor Francis had selected his other victims, usually in the first grade, and named them to be the queen of the Spring Carnival. Terrie Light, now the Northern California director of the Survivors Network of those Abused by Priests, or SNAP, had been abused by Francis twenty years before I was. She was the first sexual abuse victim of Francis to come forward. Several other women have since come forward to acknowledge Francis sexually abused them in the years between Terrie and me. So far, I am the youngest who has come forward.

My heavy abuse started when Monsignor Francis called my mother in May of 1979 and asked if she thought I would like to go out for dinner with him on Friday. My mom replied, "Oh, she would probably like that." And so I went out with him for dinner. My mother let me go. After all, I was going out with a Catholic priest. How could there be any harm in that? From then on I went out almost every other Friday night for dinner with him. And every other Sunday night he had dinner at our house. My parents enjoyed having Monsignor Francis for dinner in their home. I remember them talking about how they thought Francis missed having children and grandchildren.

I don't have any memories of the actual sequence when he first abused me. But I do remember the routine I had to follow to visit him after school in his little suite. This had been added onto the back of the rectory when Monsignor Francis had the church and rectory built. This gave him a private entrance to his living area. He told me how important it was that I not be seen entering his apartment, so I had to walk around the neighborhood until everyone in the area had left. Then I would let myself in via the side gate, and walk through his garage into his bedroom. Once inside his bedroom I would remove my underwear and unbutton my blouse.

He would already be in bed, waiting for me. After I had removed my panties and unbuttoned my blouse I would have to get into bed with him to take a nap—in quotes, "a nap."

I remember him touching my private areas with his hands, and then I remember going home. A lot of my memories of this period have gaps. But I do remember some things.

At first, when he was abusing me, he would say things to me like, "This is what love is. You like this, don't you?" Then he would tell me he loved me and ask if I loved him. I would have to say, "Yes, I love you." If I didn't, he would hurt me.

My mother took a picture of Monsignor Francis kissing me. We were at my godmother's house and for some reason Monsignor Francis was there, too. My mother thought it was a cute picture. What she didn't know, at that time, was that he had already taught me how to French kiss him. That picture, of Monsignor Francis kissing me, had been taken as part of the publicity for the Spring Carnival, the year I was queen. This was the year before he started taking me out to dinner.

Monsignor Francis started taking me for overnight trips when I was in the second grade. With my parents' permission, of course. I remember going to see the California State Fair in Sacramento and the railroad museum. I had remembered these trips as only week-end trips until I read a postcard describing one of them. He had taken me for a week-long trip to Sacramento. Here he had gotten physically violent with me.

We were staying in a hotel in Sacramento. He forced me to take a shower with him. After the shower he used a towel to dry me off. I remember he used his hands in my private areas. Then he told me to go to bed.

After I was in bed and pretending I was asleep, he came over to the bed and tied my hands and feet to the bed. Then he pulled my nightgown up over my head and raped me.

Afterward, after he had finished with me, he got up and left the room for a while. When he returned he told me I was evil and the devil's child because I had made a priest sin. Then he went through some kind of a weird ritual to cleanse me. I was still tied to the bed, because I had to be cleansed of my sins. He walked around me, chanting some words and rubbing my body, including my private parts, to cleanse me. After I was cleansed he untied me and I had to go to sleep.

The next morning, I banished the memory from my conscious mind. My body hurt, but I did not want to know why.

Monsignor Francis also took me on day trips to Santa Cruz as well as the longer trips to Sacramento. At the time, my mother told me later, she did not worry about it. But once, in 1989, when Terrie Light started picketing the Church and talking about being sexually abused

Jennifer's Story

by Francis, my mom started wondering about one particular trip I had been taken on by him. It was the last trip I ever went on with Francis. He took me to Sacramento for an overnight stay in a motel. When I returned home and my mother went to wash the nightgown I had worn on the trip, she found a pubic hair. I certainly did not have any pubic hair myself. I was still too young.

I remember my mother checking my private areas for any signs of irritation or redness. It was so embarrassing to me to be examined that way. But even as I was standing there, embarrassed about being examined, I wondered if she would be able to tell he was abusing me. But she found nothing that alarmed her, and I was still unable to speak about what Monsignor Francis was doing to me.

Yet, my mother told me, years later, that even as she was questioning what could have happened in Sacramento she also remembered that Francis was a priest. If my mother were to accuse Monsignor Francis of molesting her daughter, who in the parish would believe her?

My father was never told of my being sexually molested by a Catholic priest. He died before I told my mother. My father had devoted much of his life to the Knights of Columbus, a major Catholic men's organization. Discovering that the priest he honored and admired had sexually molested his daughter would have been devastating to him.

I still remember the first time Francis used his fingers to penetrate me. When he had tried to penetrate me with his penis he could not. Not at that time, but he did later. I have wondered since if he masturbated himself when he could not penetrate me with his penis.

When he first started to sexually abuse me, I protested. His response was to pinch my nipples. Hard. Then he told me I was not to move and I was not to cry or make any noise. If I did, he told me he would pinch me harder. It would hurt more, he said.

I believe the memories of being hurt when I showed any emotion or reacted to pain have resulted in my suppressing my emotions. At my brother's funeral some years later, I cried only because I felt I was expected to cry. At my father's funeral, I honestly cried.

It is difficult for some people to understand how I could have been so abused and my parents knew nothing about it. Monsignor Francis was so involved in our family life that I don't think my parents ever had a suspicious thought in their minds about his spending so much time with me. He became one of our family. Here is a good illustration.

In 1982, my brother-in-law was stationed in Pearl Harbor, Hawaii, with the US Navy. My parents took my brother and me to visit my sister and her husband that summer. We stayed in Pearl City at first, and then moved to the Princess Kaiulani Hotel at Waikiki

Beach for a few nights. Monsignor Francis went to Hawaii with us.

One night, while we were at the Princess Kaiulani, Francis took me to stay in his hotel room. To give my parents a break, he told them. This was the summer after my second grade in school.

He made me look at him while he was naked in the shower. I remember that time, because it was the first time he made me have oral sex on him.

The hard-core sexual abuse continued through the summer after my fourth grade. Two things happened that led to my taking a stand against his continued abuse of me. One was physical and one was psychological.

My period started on the first or second day of the fifth grade. I was real embarrassed, and very conscious of my physical body. Much more so than I had been prior to the start of my period.

At the same time they were having a lot of public service announcements on TV, which they don't seem to have anymore. These announcements talked about inappropriate touching of someone's body. This made me feel odd about what was going on. It made me feel worse than I had felt before about what Monsignor Francis was doing to me. Soon after I started the fifth grade, Monsignor Francis called my mother to see if I wanted to take a back-to-school trip to Sacramento with him. My mother put the phone down and asked me if I wanted to go. I replied in an emphatic NO. My mother said OK, and told Monsignor Francis I didn't want to go. I left the room while she was still on the phone with him.

A short time after I said no to Francis, my mother told me he had asked her if I didn't want to go because I had started my period. If that was the reason I didn't want to go, it was not a problem. He had dealt with young girls with their first periods before.

I was embarrassed and mortified. I didn't even want my father to know when I had my period. But I told my mother that was not the reason; I just didn't want to go to Sacramento with him. She did not press me for the reason I did not want to go with him.

Once I had refused to go on a trip, I became a challenge to him. I avoided him as much as possible, and avoided being somewhere when he would be in the same location. But I could not avoid him altogether. It was a Catholic school, and we were required to go to confession at least once a month. And of course we had to go to the priests for confession.

I picked the other priest to hear my confession whenever possible. And I used the kneeler side of the confessional instead of the face-to-face side. But one time I ended up in Monsignor Francis' line for confession, and I was on the face-to-face side.

I don't remember all the details, but somehow I ended up sitting on his lap, and he raped me. Right there in the confessional. Right there in the big church he had built. Right in God's house, so to speak.

Soon after Francis raped me in the confessional, he made a comment to my mother that she told me about later. My mom had driven the carpool that day, even though I had not gone to school. I had stayed home sick, which I did an inordinate amount of time in grade school. Monsignor Francis saw my mother standing in front of the church talking with the other carpool moms and went over to her.

"I don't know why that girl won't talk to me," he said.

Before I refused to travel with him, at the start of my fifth grade, he had visited my mother. It was during the summer after my fourth grade year ended. I was still traveling with him, and he was still sexually abusing me. He called and made a lunch date with my mother. He actually invited himself over to our house for lunch. I remember my mother fixing a salad for lunch because he was coming over, and that made it a special occasion. My mother and I talked about this lunch years later, after I told her about the abuse.

During the lunch, Monsignor made what my mother thought was an odd remark. He told my mother that the chancellor from the Oakland Diocese had said there were rumors going around about him. He seemed to imply, or my mother took it that way, that the rumors involved me. Francis asked my mother if she had heard anything.

He commented to my mother that, "You know," he said, "I wouldn't harm a hair on that girl's head."

My mother said, "I know you won't. Give me his phone number and I will call him and tell him it is OK."

Monsignor quickly replied, "No, no. It is OK. I will just let him know."

That conversation has led me, my mother, my husband, and everyone I have shared it with, to think that somebody, somewhere, knew what was going on between Monsignor Francis and the little girls he spent so much time with. And it should have been obvious, because it was a pattern of his behavior for several decades.

When I was sixteen, my family moved to a forty-acre ranch near Patterson, about thirty miles east of Hayward. My mom and I had been riding horses for three years, and we moved to Patterson to accommodate the horses and our riding. This, for me, was really the start of the rest of my life.

In Patterson, I was able to repress my memories of being abused for eleven years. It was not until I started sharing my memories with my first husband, prior to our marriage, that these memories came back for me. This was the first time I was able to focus on what had happened in the past with Monsignor Francis. I had tried so hard to repress the memories of being sexually abused that I had buried them deep in my mind. As I focused on my past, a number of related memories came back to me. One involved a girl I never met.

During the time he was molesting me, he would visit another girl in Texas once or twice a year. I know he was molesting her also, but I can't tell you how I know. He had pictures of her as a young teenager in Texas and he showed them to me.

When I started talking about this abuse with my mother, I found out there had been a female parishioner with three girls from a previous marriage who had remarried and moved to Texas. When I heard about this woman and her three daughters, my first thought was "Oh my God." We have not heard from them yet. I can't help but wonder if one of the daughters was being abused by Monsignor Francis.

In August, 2000, my husband, Mike, started working as a photographer for a company that published church directories. One day when Mike returned home after working at a church he asked me if he went to a Catholic Church, would I want him to arrange an appointment with the priest to tell my story?

Because, as he told me, "They broke you, and they are going to fix you."

I agreed with Mike that I needed to tell my story if I was ever going to be healed. We decided to move ahead.

The next week, Mike visited a church in Stockton, which was the diocese we lived in, but after talking with the priest he did not feel comfortable sharing my story with him. Mike left Stockton and drove to St. Joseph's in Modesto, where he met with the young Father Joe— not the older Father Joe. Mike asked Father Joe if he could talk with him about something serious.

Father Joe replied, "Sure. Just check back with me whenever you have the time."

And Mike did go back the following week, and told Father Joe about my being sexually abused by a priest, but did not give any details. Mike came home and told me this, and said Father Joe needed my permission to inform the chancellor in Stockton.

I told Mike he had my permission to do that. We had not identified the priest at this point, but had said the abuse took place in Hayward, which is the Oakland Diocese.

The next day, or the day after, a monsignor from the Stockton Diocese called me and asked my permission to call his counterpart in the Oakland Diocese since this is where the abuse happened. I understood what he was saying. Since the abuse happened in the Oakland Diocese, they are the ones to pay for it, not the Stockton Diocese. I gave him permission, and he passed my name and phone number on to Sister Barbara Flannery of the Oakland Diocese.

Sister Barbara called me within two days, and I gave her the whole story. She promised me she would check into it and get back to me as soon as she had any more information.

Less than one week later, I received another telephone call from Sister Barbara. The first thing she told me was how she had spoken to the monsignor at Stockton about me. But she had only started describing my abuse when the monsignor stopped her. He said, "Let me guess. The abuser's name is George J. Francis." Sister Barbara told me she just said, "Oh my God."

This monsignor, who was the Stockton chancellor, told Sister Barbara to tell me not to worry about being believed. He said most people worried about not being believed when they first told their story of being abused by a priest. But he wanted Sister Barbara to tell me that I would be believed.

Sister Barbara then told me that I was not the only victim who had been sexually abused by Francis. Terrie Light was one of the victims, perhaps the first, and she had asked Sister Barbara to tell any other victims who came forward that Terrie would like to talk with them. Sister Barbara asked if she could tell my story to Terrie and give her my phone number. I was floored.

First of all, I had gone from thinking there was no one else this had ever happened to. Then there were news reports about other victims, but they were usually talking about the male victims. If I was watching TV with my mother, before I told her I had been abused, and the TV reporter started telling the audience about a priest accused of molesting young boys, my mother would turn to me and say something like: "Oh my God, did you see what this priest is accused of? I can't believe that."

And she would ask me, "Do you believe a priest would do that?" I would reply, "Yes, mother, it is bad. I have to go home now." And I would leave without discussing it any further. Or telling my mother I had been abused by that type of priest. And now, a monsignor was telling me I would be believed!

When I was telling my story to Sister Barbara, she took notes on what I was saying. Sometimes she would add a little comment to what I was telling her. For example, when I described Monsignor Francis's apartment, she made little comments that showed me she had been in that apartment and she knew I was describing it accurately.

She also asked if I had ever met his sister. Francis apparently liked taking the girls over to see his sister.

My comment was, "Was that who it was?" I could never remember if it was his sister-in-law or his sister. But I had also met his brother-in-law. His brother-in-law liked to touch and grope and feel—and kiss. His brother-in-law raped me once in Sacramento, when Monsignor Francis's sister and her husband had gone on a trip with Monsignor and me.

Francis had also taken me to visit a great aunt or grand-mother in San Francisco. I found out later he had taken another of the girls to visit this older woman in San Francisco. I guess he liked to introduce us to his family.

Anyway, I gave Sister Barbara permission to give my name and phone number to Terrie. And we soon got together to talk. But first, Sister Barbara called and said the Oakland Diocese was willing to pay for therapy for me. That was great news for us.

I had gone to see a doctor some months before when I started cutting myself severely on my arms and wrists. My husband had taken me to see the doctor, who had referred me to our insurance company psy-chologist. This was the required first step in getting referred to a therapist our insurance company would pay for. The psychologist decided I was only moder-ately depressed, and my condition could be treated on a weekly outpatient basis.

But there was a twenty-dollar co-pay per visit, and, at that point, we could not afford it. Soon afterwards, I quit my job and lost my insurance benefits. There was just no way we could afford to pay for my therapy, so the offer from the Oakland Diocese to pay for my treat-ments was welcome.

Since publicly coming out and telling my story I have talked with other survivors of Monsignor Francis. And there are many of us. We think that, if we were to back-track through all of the Carnival queens, we would probably have a pretty complete listing of his victims. My mom has told me that I didn't start going to his apartment after school until after I was the spring queen of the Carnival, which was in May of 1979.

Sister Barbara asked me if he had ever called me Princess. I told her that was his name for me. His little Princess.

When my story went public, I received an email from a woman who had been abused by Francis. This was followed by a phone call, and she told me some of the things he had done to her, and they were the same things he had done to me.

Then, soon after I held a press conference in November of 2002, two other survivors of Monsignor Francis came out publicly. One other survivor told the Oakland Diocese, but did not want to tell her story publicly nor to reveal her name. I know there are other survivors out there who have not stepped forward yet. Sister Barbara has told me there were at least six or seven girls abused by Francis.

Part of the reason I had locked those secrets away in my mind was because I was protecting my mother from death. Monsignor Francis had warned me that if I ever told anyone what he was doing to me, God would take my family. God would take someone I loved. For years I protected my mom. Not so much my dad. Some for my dad, but not as much as for my mom. I protected my mother from this knowledge for years. I did not tell her until just before I went to the attorney, in the summer of 2002. That is when I told her.

Terrie Light and I met in the winter of 2000. That was the most amazing thing to me, to meet another victim of the priest who had abused me. Terrie told me I was the third victim, including Terrie herself, to come forward to the Diocese after being abused by Francis. I was the only one who was willing to talk with Terrie about the abuse. The other lady was too fragile to handle a discussion about Francis and what he did to her.

There have been many other elements of my story of abuse by Monsignor Francis. Some of these I know I will never remember. And I am not the only victim who has blocked out memories of him. After I went public, a lady from a bank in Hayward, who had been at Saint Bede's as a girl, called to tell Terrie Light her story. She remembers Francis taking the little girls out for donuts. None of them wanted to go, but they could not refuse. She remembers she did not like going with him, but that is all she remembers. And when your mind blocks things out, there is a reason it is doing that.

When I filed my law suit, at the press conference in November of 2003, several people told me they were surprised I had filed so soon. My therapist thought I was still a couple of years away from being able to publicly deal with the abuse. Terrie Light told me she thought I would never be able to file. And even my husband Mike was surprised I filed. But I had decided it was time.

I am still in therapy, and I am still healing. I think about the sexual abuse I went through and wonder why he picked me. It doesn't even seem like it was for sex. It was more for control and dominance.

If there was one question I could ask of the Church and all its leaders, it would be this: "Why are you listening to what the lawyers tell you what to do and not what God tells you to do? How can it be right for the Church to lie when God says you are never to lie?"

My last comment concerns the Church itself. I don't know if the Church will ever reform, especially since the ones who would have to do the reforming are the same priests and bishops who have sexually abused children and then covered up the abuses by themselves and their fellow priests. But the Church is not a safe place for children today, because there are still abusive priests in the ranks.

Steve's Story

Editor's Comments

Steve's story was difficult for me to place in proper perspective. The single incident Steve describes as the original abuse by a priest seemed, at first, minor in nature. It was not until I understood the impact this incident had on a ten-year-old boy that I realized it was not a minor incident, but the defining moment in Steve's life.

The feelings of inadequacy and powerlessness Steve felt with Towle as a ten-year-old boy continued to play a major role in his dealings, as a college student, with other Jesuit priests. The initial pattern, established by Towle, was to continue.

I discovered, as I interviewed more and more sexual survivors, that the impact of sexual abuse on their lives went far beyond any physical damage they suffered. The psychological and emotional damage each sexual survivor suffered at the hands of the priests left mental and emotional scars that persisted decades after the physical scars may have healed. The psychological conditions established by the abuse have lead to feelings of vulnerability, a sense of low self esteem and self worth, and the potential for the survivor to continue to view himself as a victim.

Against this background, it is interesting and unique to hear why Steve declined to sue the Catholic Church. He felt it was more important to him to know he could provide for himself, without any large cash settlement from the Catholic Church, than to have the financial security such a settlement might have provided.

It should also be noted that Steve had sexual relationships with four Jesuit priests. It seems difficult to believe that these four were the only Jesuit priests who preyed on students for sexual gratification. Steve reported the incidents to the Jesuit authorities and received a mixed response in return. The general tenor of the letters sent to Steve by the Jesuits indicated that it was not considered an important occurrence to them.

Perhaps the strongest lesson from Steve's story is his willingness to accept personal responsibility for his healing. He can see that his problems were caused by and exacerbated by priests, but he is determined to resolve his issues himself. He knows the priests were part of his problem. They cannot be part of his solution.

Here is Steve's story as he told it to me, sitting in the backyard of his San Francisco home. The sun was shining, we were drinking tea, and we seemed a long way away from the abuse he described. Yet the abuse was right there, in every way as real to Steve then as the day he was abused.

I grew up in the village of Sea Cliff, which is a little village on the north shore of Long Island in New York. It is only a mile square, right on the coast about twenty miles from Manhattan. I grew up learning to swim in the sound. There were two Russian Orthodox Churches, one on either end of our village. I went to mass at St. Boniface Martyr and attended the St. Boniface Martyr Grade School.

My family had a two-story, four-bedroom house, number 77 on Ransom Avenue. My father would eventually remodel the basement into a bedroom where my mother lived in later years, after their marriage started falling apart. When my grandmother started slowing down, my parents had a small apartment built over the two-car garage in the back. When I say we had a small apartment built, I really mean my father built the apartment with the help of a friend of his who did the electrical work. Here my grandmother lived for the last years of her life.

My childhood home was not a fancy house. It had a little front yard with the garage in the back. We had hardly any back yard. A driveway circled the house, ending at the garage. It was a good family home for us. My mother just recently sold this home after living in it for more than forty-eight years.

My family consisted of my mother and father, Jake the oldest son, and Alex and Tim, who are older than me. I also have two sisters. Mary is older and Roseanne, the baby of the family, is younger.

I slept in the upstairs, where the abuse by Father Towle took place. The upstairs bedrooms were really a converted attic. My father had made one large bedroom out of the attic and then placed a divider in the middle. This divider was just a bookshelf halfway across the room and did not reach the ceiling. It served as a means of making two bedrooms out of one room with a semblance of privacy.

I was ten years old when Father Towle, S.J., or Society of Jesus, abused me. I slept in one part of the attic bedroom. My brothers Alex and Tim slept on the other side when they were home. At that time, both were in college and seldom home. The oldest son in the family, my brother Jake, had enlisted in the US Air Force and was not around much.

Downstairs were two bedrooms. My parents slept in one. My two sisters shared the smaller room.

If I go back in time, to before I was ten years old, I shared the bedroom with Mary downstairs before Roseanne was born. After her birth, I was moved upstairs with the other boys. I remember my mother would sometimes read stories to me from the lives of the saints or Bible stories. She would give us books as presents or check out books from the library for us. She liked us to read in the living room. But, with six children, she never had much time to sit down and read stories to us or to listen to us read to her. She was just too busy.

In 1969, my parents went on a marriage encounter retreat. They followed up on this retreat by attending classes at Inisfada, a Jesuit retreat house in Manhasset, Long Island. It was at Inisfada that they met Father Joseph Towle, a Jesuit priest. My mother recalls she had two individual sessions with Father Towle and a joint counseling session with my father. My parents were going through a difficult time in their lives and thought counseling from the Catholic priests and attending the retreats would help them with their marriage.

The Jesuit priests from Inisfada frequently visited our local parish, St Boniface Martyr, to be guest celebrants at Sunday mass. I am certain Towle did this at least once.

At the time, Towle was perhaps forty-five or so. Of course to me, at ten years old, he was old like my parents were old. Towle was younger than my father. He was trim and in very good physical shape. He had a quiet, soft presence about him, one of infinite patience. My mother introduced him to me. She was happy for a priest to meet her children and overjoyed for her son to have the opportunity to be with a priest.

My mother told us children that, after Towle saw my father in the counseling session, his diagnosis for him was "as if emotionally he was mentally retarded." His emotions, or lack of emotions, would never allow him to be the loving husband my mother wanted.

It should come as no surprise that my father made it known he did not like Towle. Did not like him at all. It was also about this time my parents stopped sharing a bedroom. My mother said she found herself much happier when my father was out of the house.

Affection was important to my mother, but it was something that had eluded her all of her life. She grew up in a home she described as vacant of warmth and affection from her parents. Her classmates teased her for being Roman Catholic, so she turned to the parish priests for acceptance and attention. She went to confession out of loneliness.

With this in her earliest childhood and teenage years, it should not be surprising that she developed an absolute love for priests, especially Jesuit priests. She thought they were the smartest, holiest priests of all. They read books and taught. She had an absolute feeling of respect, love, and devotion for these priests.

My mother's love of Jesuit priests greatly influenced my perception of them. Up until I was in my early twenties, I wanted to be a missionary priest. My first summer in college, at Fordham, I traveled with a group of students to Mexico to build houses for the poor. At confirmation, I took the name Damien in honor of Father Joseph de Veuster, the leper priest of Molokai.

Going back to my mother's childhood explains the role Father Towle was able to play in my life. My mother grew up with parents who didn't know how to give or receive affection. This made my mother insecure about being affectionate. In addition, her mother-in-law was a constant presence in our family life. She always stayed with us on holidays and many weekends as well. She chided my mother for her lack of affection to her children. My mother, out of spite, responded by giving even less physical affection to her children.

This lack of affection—physical, mental, and emotional—from my parents resulted in my being starved for any kind of attention and affection. When Towle gave me his attention and affection, I greedily accepted. This is part of the reason why his betrayal hurt me so deeply.

And that brings me to the incident of abuse.

It was around 1971. My father was working in Boston, coming home to Long Island every other weekend. He did this, while working for Texaco, for more than two years. It seemed he was seldom home. My older brothers were away. Tim was at Cornell and Alex was staying with our grandmother in Manhattan while he attended Cooper Union. Jake was in the Air Force.

Towle was either invited by my mother to stay at our house or he had requested staying there. He had moved from Long Island to Staten Island, but continued to make visits and conduct lectures on Long

Island. When he was on Long Island, he would frequently stay with us.

One night, soon after my first meeting with Towle, he came to stay overnight with us. The upstairs bedrooms were empty except for mine. After dinner, Father Towle and I went upstairs to go to bed. I was moved to the "guest" bedroom portion of the attic bedroom so I could sleep in the same room as Father Towle.

I should explain some of the circumstances of the feelings I had for Towle at the time. He had made me feel like I was special to him. His letters to my mother would always include a little message for me. After reading his letters, my mother would always tell me, "Father Towle asked about you." Or "Father Towle said to give you his love." I really felt I had a special friend in Father Towle, someone who was special, like all priests are special, and who thought I was special. And, of course, my mother was thrilled that a priest was paying attention to me.

Towle cultivated this feeling that I was special to him. The first night I met him, when he came over to our house for dinner, he let me read to him. My mother was in the kitchen cooking up a special meal for our special guest. Father Towle and I were alone in the living room.

We sat next to each other on the sofa. I read Dr. Seus's *Bartholomew Cummings and The 500 Hats*. I wasn't a good reader. I didn't think I could read the whole book by myself, but with Towle's help I did. His patience and gentleness overwhelmed me. I could make mistakes or struggle infinitely, and it wasn't too much for him to sit through. He just sat on the sofa besides me, patient and caring. When he helped me finish the reading, I had a new sense of accomplishment and self-pride. I was very much in love, as a son loves his father, with this new man who more than made up for the absence of my own father. What I felt strongest was that Towle loved me and thought me special.

After the two of us had gone upstairs to the bedroom, but before actually going to bed, Towle had me undress so he could give me a back rub. This massage included my buttocks. I remember he commented on how chunky my buttocks were. The massage he gave me lasted a substantial period of time. It must have been fifteen minutes, or maybe even half an hour. I am not sure of the length of time, I just know I was uncomfortable. The massage seemed to go on and on.

Towle finished my massage and told me to massage him. He had taken his clothes off and he was nude. And I was nude, as he had directed. My sense of powerlessness was complete. I remember attempting to do just as he had done to me except his buttocks. When I felt I could do no more, Towle specifically asked me to massage his buttocks. I could not say no. I had to trust that this man knew best. I did not want to lose his love for me or my sense of being special to him.

This experience was emotionally painful. I didn't want to believe this man, who I loved and wanted to be loved by, was doing this to me. With fear and dread also came a sense of inadequacy and failure—failure that I had not massaged him properly, inadequacy that something was wrong inside of me for having the feelings I had. I remember how uncomfortable I was about my nakedness, how uncomfortable I was about his nakedness, how uncomfortable I was to have him massage my buttocks and then to make his comment on how chunky I was, and especially how uncomfortable I was when forced to massage his buttocks.

Offsetting these feelings of failure, inadequacy, and discomfort were the feelings I had enjoyed when we sat together on the sofa and he listened while I read Dr. Seus. He always hugged me when he said hello or goodbye. I loved that feeling of closeness with him. That was the first and only time I was alone with Towle in our home.

I remember one evening shortly after the massage incident. Towle arrived at our home early one evening. It was still light outside and much too early for my bedtime but, as soon as I heard my mother greet him, I jumped into bed and faked being asleep. My mother called upstairs to me, but I did not answer. I remember thinking how surprised she must have been. She would think I would love to see Towle. She would not understand why I had gone to bed so early.

— Steve's Story—

My mother continued to stay in touch with Towle, but I never wanted to see him alone again. I did see him every few years or so at a public function. We never talked together during this period. But, in spite of my fear of seeing him alone, he remained my role model. Perhaps this was partly due to my confusion over what he had done to me and my feelings for him. It was also partly because I still looked up to him as a priest. He was the main reason I selected Fordham University to go to college, since he was teaching there. I felt I had to resolve this confusion in my mind over my feelings for him and what he had done. The only way to do that was to confront him.

When I read these words, they sound foolish. Foolish now, when I read them as an adult. But, when I was ten, and then through my high school years, these feelings were a dominant part of my life—these feelings and the resulting confusion in my emotions.

When I was in the fifth grade, I remember sitting in class attempting to make myself invisible. I sat in the back of the room and kept my face behind the head of my classmate in front of me, between me and the teacher, Ms. Goldsboro. At a point halfway through the year Ms. Goldsboro looked at me with a puzzled expression. She asked who I was. I had successfully hidden myself for half the year.

I am now, as an adult, suspicious of my avoidance behavior. Had I learned from Towle not to draw attention to myself for fear of the repercussions? It was for Towle I opened up. I read for him with newfound pride. I hugged, shared affection, and loved him only to be betrayed. His actions bluntly informed me I was not to be loved for my person or my brilliant reading, only for my ass. His comment about how chunky my ass was has always stayed with me.

Also, about this time, another occurrence stands out. I started having daily headaches and a general feeling of sadness. I reported this to my mother. I remember taking a couple of weeks off from school, getting attention from my mother, and going to an eye clinic, a family doctor, and to a neurologist. The doctors found nothing physically wrong with me. At the end of the two weeks, with all the attention I had received, I suddenly felt better and the headaches went away.

A feeling of sadness did not stay away. I remember acting out a fake suicide. I emptied an aspirin bottle and wrote a note stating how sad I was. I waited for my mother to find me in bed, eyes closed and groggy with sleep. An empty aspirin bottle clasped in my hand. I can still recall how concerned my mother was. She was so compassionate.

Later, in the eighth grade, I remember bursting into tears for no specific reason. When the teacher asked me why, I didn't have a clue.

Now, as an adult looking back in time, I believe there is a connection between these incidents and what Towle did to me. I was reacting directly to his betrayal. This resulted in my being depressed and mistrustful of others. I went to great lengths to avoid being noticed and I did not want to be special to anyone, since I knew the pain being special could cause.

In high school, I found I had to work hard to maintain a B average. I look back in amazement at how lacking I was in any sense of self. I played sports and excelled at Lacrosse. Despite enjoying practice more than game competition, I found myself nominated in my senior year as team captain and MVP.

When it came time for me to pick a college, I looked at several schools with lacrosse teams, but lacrosse was not really a major consideration. I chose Fordham, which had no lacrosse team or even a lacrosse club. What Fordham had was Towle, who was the provincial of the Jesuit novices. I think if I had been asked at that time who my hero was, I would have replied Father Joseph Towle—even after he abused me.

The lore related to him was that he had worked with tough street youths. He was fearless, kind, and gentle. He was for superpower disarmament and peace. I had kept him always in my mind and in my heart. Yet in spite of these feelings of respect and love, I also had tremendous feelings toward him of hurt and confusion.

During my five years at Fordham, I had maybe three encounters with Towle, and this was in spite of the fact he was the reason I selected Fordham. I think now I didn't seek to interact more with him due to a healthy fear and knowledge that he would hurt me more, and also the thought that he was not the one who could answer my questions and help me solve my confusion. He was the one who had created my problems and confusion. He would not be the one to help me reach a solution.

But not seeing Towle while at Fordham did not mean I was not meeting other Jesuit priests, who only added to my sexual confusion.

In the summer of 1987, I visited my family in New York and some of my friends. I also called Towle and asked if I could visit him. He was working at a parish in the South Bronx and arranged for me to meet him at his residence. He gave me a tour of the neighborhood and took me to an Italian restaurant. Towle was obviously well known at the restaurant. When we finished, we were told a local politician had already paid our bill. Towle was not surprised to hear this. He seemed to think that was his due.

We walked back to his residence and went to his room. We both sat on his bed, in almost complete darkness, and neither of us said or did anything. I felt discomfort, awkwardness and confusion. Something was missing. Neither of us brought up the subject of the massage incident at my home. I left with no greater understanding of our relationship than when I arrived. Towle had not given me an apology nor an explanation for his behavior. It was as if it had never happened.

The last time I saw Towle was during the summer of 1992. I was visiting a friend in the Bronx. We went swimming at the Lombardi Sports Center. After swimming, I was sitting in the sauna when Towle walked in and sat adjacent to me. I made no eye contact with him and he seemed not to notice or recognize me. He had two Latino grade-school boys with him. The presence of the two Latino boys, of the same age I had been when Towle molested me, brought back painful memories. But I was unable to confront Towle in public. I left the sauna as quickly as I could.

That evening, I found myself upset. I had been in therapy for two years and the issue of my discomfort during the massage incident had been discussed. I was questioning whether the massage incident had been sexual molestation. Seeing Towle with two young boys prompted me to call New York State Central Registry of Child Abuse, Department of Social Services, and to write to the Jesuits. I also decided I had to bring this to the attention of the Jesuits. This is what I wrote.

June 21, 1992
Reverend Joseph Parkes, S.J.
Kolhman Hall
501 E. Fordham Road
Bronx, New York 10458

Dear Reverend Parkes:

*I write to you to make a complaint of sexual moles-
tation by Father Joseph Towle, S.J. and to request
that it be promptly addressed.*

*A single incident of sexual assault and molestation
happened somewhere between the years 1968 and
1971 when I was between the ages of seven and ten.
At the time Fr. Towle acted as a spiritual advisor
and marriage counselor to my mother. A trust was
developed as to where Fr. Towle could stay overnight if he wished.*

*It is only now that I have found the clarity and the
courage to make this report. Three years of psychotherapy have helped unravel confusion, pain, and
anger.*

*It is my understanding (see attached article on
bishops confront sexual abuse) that you wish the
report of any such incident and that you are anx-
ious to properly address it.*

*I do wish to be informed as to the result of this
report.*

*If I can be of more assistance, please do not hesi-
tate to contact me.*

Sincerely,
Stephen Roberts.

At the same time I contacted the NY State Central Registry of Child Abuse, Department of Social Services.

Even though I was not as clear or certain as I am now that Towle was wrong to do what he did to me, I still felt I had to protect those children from possible harm. Seeing the two young boys with Towle made me aware that someone had to stop Towle from abusing other boys as he had abused me. I decided to take that responsibility to alert the Jesuits.

During the 1982 school year at Fordham, I got involved with Pax Christi, a newly formed campus club. I became friends with two members, John Yassenchek, S.J., and Michael _____, S.J., two scholastics. In May, 1982, through these two priests, I was introduced to Father James Janda, S.J.

The next time I saw Father Janda, I was walking around the campus. We exchanged greetings as we passed.

The third time we met, he invited several of us over to his room. Besides myself, there was Margaret Egan (my girlfriend at the time), Michael (a fellow student), a Jesuit priest, and Stan (also a fellow student). We all walked over to his room at Kohlmann Hall. There we drank beer. Janda smoked pot. We drew colored pictures and ate some fruit. As it grew late, past midnight, Margaret and Stan had to leave. As it grew later, Michael had to leave. So there were just the two of us, Father Janda and myself.

Janda was wild, irreverent, and funny. I could tell he was taken with me. He was the life of the party. During a game we had earlier played, blindfolds on, we had shared an apple. Janda cheated, lifted his blind fold and kissed me passionately on the lips. It was the first time I had ever been kissed by a man. I was surprised. I did not like it, but felt absolutely helpless to say no.

I knew I liked Janda; that he was funny, wild, an artist, a poet, had published poetry, taught second grade, did theater in Manhattan, and he was a Jesuit. What I liked best was that he liked me and thought I was somebody. Even though it was not on my agenda to be kissed by Janda, I would suffer that to be liked. I trusted Janda to know what was best for me.

So that night, after Michael left, I stayed because I knew Janda wanted me to. We stayed up all night. Janda started by giving me a massage. He removed my shoes and sox and started with my feet. He gradually took off more of my clothing, and his, as he continued to massage me. He continued until he was giving me a full body massage. Finally he massaged my genitals. I had my first orgasm. To say that I did not experience intense pleasure would be a lie. Right after my orgasm, I told Janda I thought he was God.

Sometime during this night, I told Janda about the discomfort I had felt when Towle had massaged me. His reaction was that Towle had done wrong. He told me the worst homophobes were the most closeted homosexuals.

I did not go back to see Janda for months. I was still digesting the experience. For me, the prize again was that someone wonderful, powerful, important—a Jesuit—wanted me. Also it was a revelation for me that men could be sexual with each other. I looked at my relationships in a new light. I saw my girlfriend as weak and demure. I saw my friend Paul as strong, intelligent, and Jesuit-trained at Regis.

On Memorial Day of 1992, I initiated a sexual relationship with Paul. Paul had recently broken up with his girlfriend. I acted out with Paul all I had recently learned from Janda. I ended my relationship with Margaret. Paul and I soon moved in with each other and became closeted lovers. My relationship with Paul lasted seven years and instigated my move to San Francisco.

Soon after my sexual encounter with Janda, he was transferred to Denver, Colorado. Six months later, he came back to visit New York. He invited me to meet his Jesuit friend Billie McNichols, S.J., and stay overnight at Billie's Brooklyn apartment. I did stay overnight and remember a sleepless night fighting off sexual advances from Janda.

In addition to my sexual encounter with Janda, I met Herb Rogers, S.J., a retired Fordham professor. We became friends while I was a Fordham student. We would take long walks on campus, talking about a number of topics. But, after he gave me a French kiss and grabbed my buttocks, I no longer felt any trust towards him. Rogers was three times my age, and I had no physical attraction to him. I wondered why Rogers would think I wanted him to kiss me? I had never said or done anything, consciously, to indicate I wanted any type of a sexual relationship with him.

During our long walks around campus, I told Rogers about Janda. Rogers had spent time at a Manhattan parish where my mother attended services. He told her I was generous, but also confused. I believe my confusion stemmed from the power imbalance in my relationship with the priests. I looked for trust and attention, while it seemed they sought sexual gratification at my expense.

The fourth and last Jesuit I had sexual relations with was closer to my own age, perhaps ten years older. I had already graduated from Fordham with a B.A. in combined social sciences with a concentration in social work. I met Peter Sui, S.J., while we were both riding the subway. I was living in Bedford Park, the next neighborhood up from the campus. We were taking the subway, the D train, up to Fordham Road. He told me he was a baby Jesuit living on campus. He invited me to his residence on campus, in McCauley Hall.

I walked to his residence with him. When we arrived, he invited me in. That evening he played the piano for me. He told me he was a lawyer. I thought he was a very good piano player. He looked very young, effeminate, and very Asian. After he played the piano for a while, we said goodnight and I left. He seemed very interested in me, and I gave him my phone number—or he gave me his phone number, I am not sure now. In any case we met again. One night, he came over to my apartment in the Bronx. We both got nude and rubbed our bodies together. He showed me what to do, how to put his penis between my legs and masturbate him that way. That was the last time I saw Sui in New York.

I did see him again in San Francisco several years later. We had a mutual friend living in San Francisco. This man, a graduate student from the Bronx I had stayed in touch with, told me stories about Peter Sui and how sexually provocative he was. I think this is how I learned Sui was in San Francisco.

In any case, I met Sui and we spent an afternoon together. We drove over to Baker Beach, near San Francisco. Sui was very excited about seeing the nude part of Baker Beach. But it was a short visit, and I didn't get together with him again.

I did have an unusual incident with Sui that I reported to the Jesuits. There did not seem to be any interest on their part in determining if Sui was sexually seeking other men. There was no interest in a follow-on investigation of any type by the Jesuit provincials.

In 1992, after sending the letter about Towle to Father Parkes, S.J., I decided to tell my mother. It seems strange now, but I had never considered telling her before. There was such a strong sense, on my part, of rationalization; I believed that Father Towle was absolutely correct and attempting to help me. I had wanted to believe he had tried to give me physical healing, a healing touch, that he had been touching me out of compassion and love.

At first, she could not understand how I could have stayed in contact with him after the abuse. Then she asked, "Did he penetrate you?" I told her no.

My mother made an appointment with Father Towle and went over to see him. She told me about her meeting afterwards.

She had told Towle of my accusations. According to my mother Towle had responded by saying, "I never meant to do anything wrong." Then my mother and Towle had prayed together and that was that. As far as my mother was concerned, the subject was over and forgotten. She continued to go to church every day and continued her friendships with the priests. She asked me to pray with her, and talked about forgiveness and letting things go. She could not accept how important this was to me, how traumatic it had been, and how much it had affected my life.

My mother's reaction to Towle molesting me was a disappointment. I don't know what I expected her to do, but for her to react as if nothing had happened was hurtful to me. It was as if it didn't matter to her what Towle had done, while to me it mattered a great deal.

It was a different story when I told my father. By the time I told him, the same summer I told my mother, he and my mother were living separate lives. My mother had moved to the basement in our family home, which had been renovated as a separate apartment. My father continued to sleep in the bedroom on the main floor. He had stopped going to mass. I think he had been going because my mother wanted him to. Once their marriage turned sour, he didn't see any reason or need to go to mass.

I can still remember how it was when I told my dad about Towle. Dad had picked me up from the airport. We were driving home along the Long Island Expressway. On the way I told him I had been molested by Father Towle, a man he had never liked. I can still see his reaction, a tearful grimace. I could see it was painful for him to hear this.

His reaction was strikingly different from my mother's. My father showed, and expressed, a great deal more compassion then my mother had. But it was also somewhat disappointing for both of us because I knew my father was too old and sick to avenge me or act in a powerful way. He seemed to realize that too. All he could do was to share his grief and sorrow with me. My father became very sick shortly after I told him. He developed pancreatic cancer and died in 1993.

Seeing Towle with the two Latino boys in the sauna left a deep impression on me, and made me determined to stop him from molesting other boys as he had molested me. I had hoped the letter I sent to Father Parkes in 1992 would be sufficient for this purpose, but I became disappointed at the lack of response I received. It took me months to get an answer from Parkes. Our initial phone conversation was during normal working hours, and I was at my desk at the office. I felt uncomfortable talking about a priest and me being nude together. I was afraid some of my coworkers would overhear my side of the conversation. I think Father Parkes made some sort of apology in this conversation, but I was so nervous I am not sure what was said.

I finally had a face-to-face meeting with Father Parkes in New York City. It was not what I had expected. Father Parkes started by telling me it was his job to take care of the priests and protect them. This was a difficult, time-consuming task. I remember thinking I really didn't care about his troubles with wayward priests. I was concerned with only the wayward priest who had molested me and caused me so much emotional damage. Father Parkes also made the comment that most pedophiles are married men, so it is not just priests molesting children. This was beside the point of our discussion. He also told me there were no other incidents of molestation that had been brought against Father

Towle. He claimed Father Towle had undergone some psychological testing.

Then Father Parkes informed me that the other two Jesuits, Sui and Janda, were in other provinces. He really couldn't address their case. I asked for the name and address of someone in their provinces so I could send a letter regarding these two priests, and I did send letters. I never felt I received any indication of interest on the part of the Jesuits regarding these two priests— or Towle, for that matter.

I decided to seek financial restitution. I was not looking for financial security for the rest of my life. I was not even interested in making the Jesuits pay for the mental and emotional damage I felt Towle had caused me. I decided I would ask the Jesuits to pay the actual costs of my therapy to date and the travel expenses I had in- curred in pursuing a clarification of my situation. To substantiate my claim I wrote up what I called "My Memoir." In this, I detailed what had happened, to the best of my ability. This memoir is the basis for my story here. I should add that I had already paid the bills that I was requesting reimbursement for. I was not seeking punitive damages. The expenses I listed were:

$24,750	Therapy.
$ 970	Travel costs.
$ 385	Conferences and Membership fees in SNAP
$26,105	

On May 17, 1995, I received a letter from the New York Province of the Society of Jesus. Father George Driscoll, S.J., wrote:

Dear Mr. Roberts:

Thank you for the letter containing your "memoir" and the other materials you sent.

I have passed these materials on to Father Parkes, the provincial to whom you wrote and spoke in 1992. I can assure you that he is in the process of addressing your concerns.

I understand your predicament, and you have my prayers for continued healing.

Sincerely yours,
(Rev.) George F. Driscoll,
S.J. Provincial Assistant

A variety of meetings, phone calls, and letters produced an agreement.

I received a letter from Mangialardi & Berardino, Attorneys at Law. The letter was dated December 27, 1995. They agreed to pay the bills I had submitted in full, provided I signed a complete release. The letter said:

Dear Mr. Roberts,

After meeting with Father Parkes and being given copies of the bills you submitted to him I have prepared a release for you to sign before a notary public. This release should be signed in duplicate and initialed by you on each page and then returned to me in the enclosed envelope. Upon my receipt of said release a check for $26,105.00 (twenty-six thousand one hundred five dollars and no cents) will be forwarded to you.

If you have any questions concerning the release please contact me at your earliest convenience.

Very truly yours,
/s/ Michael S. Berardino MB: lb
Cc: New York Province Society of Jesus
    Father Parkes

I signed the release and had it notarized. On January 30, 1996, Mr. Berardino sent me another letter, this time with a check enclosed for $26,105.00.

I have been asked why I hadn't sued and why I settled for just reimbursement of the actual costs I had incurred and paid. Why didn't I go after future therapy costs and punitive damages?

This is a complicated question. I started off by approaching the Jesuits and wanting restitution, but I am not even sure what that word means technically. I wanted amends made in all areas where I felt I had been damaged—my relationship with my mother, my relationship with my father, my relationship with my best friend at Fordham (Paul King), the relationships I had later in my life, my wife (actually my ex-wife now)—just the people in my life. I ran up the whole bill, and, after I negotiated with Rev. Parkes in person, in Manhattan, I needed to take a huge step back and think what would be a positive first step forward for me.

The first step I had to take was to bring the issue real close to home—to just talk about myself, to focus on me, and how it has been a struggle to understand what happened with the priests and myself, to understand what happened in the bedroom with Father Towle. The key part of understanding was the therapy I did in San Francisco. I decided limiting the claim for restitution to the actual therapy costs was a good first step.

Also I realized that the Jesuits weren't the complete, end-all story of my life. They are not the only reason I am in therapy. It is not the only struggle in life I have had. Not my only difficulty.

And I thought, what is the price that I would pay? If I were to take more money from the Jesuits, or to ask for more money, does it have the sort of meaning that I can't do for myself—or that I need this help from the

Jesuits? I want to be clear in my life that I am independent. I can take care of my own needs. I don't need their help. Does that mean the $26,000 they reimbursed me for therapy costs covered all the damage that was done or the difficulties that were caused? I am not sure about that. So it is a complicated issue. I am not sure how to answer it completely.

Other friends have asked me what I lost because of the initial abuse by Towle. This caused me to look at the situation I find myself in now. First of all, I want to try and move ahead in my life and take responsibility for what is mine. I also realize that the incident has made me aware of many things that people are not normally aware of. It has given me an understanding, in a way, of the struggles I have today with intimacies, with relationships, and with my family.

I have examined the concept of what I "lost" with each of the priests I was sexually involved with. Towle helped me with my reading, and then abused me. After that incident it was difficult for me to have a sense of confidence in my abilities. With the other priests, I was taught that life was about seduction and sex. Their sexual dealings with me created a difficult pattern for me to move away from. That, I think, makes it difficult for me to develop intimate, trusting relationships.

I was once asked what was the most important element in my story. I replied that at some point I realized I had to choose to move forward—to find ways to heal myself, to accept what happened, to continue to try and move ahead, to not hold onto it as an explanation for everything bad that happens in my life. It is like a death in the family or a broken love affair. There is a tremendous loss associated with dramatic events in our lives, but somehow we have to find things we care about and continue living. It is that process of growing that allows us to move on.

And there is one more aspect of this abuse I would like to mention. I am almost forty-two years old and something that happened to me when I was ten and then in my early twenties is still a major part of my life. It took me until I was in my thirties to even look back and start to understand the incident. It takes that long to understand something and to put it in its place and deal with it. It is a similar situation to what I have seen working with Vietnam veterans. They have been having nightmares for twenty years and have no way of dealing with the nightmares except for drugs and hurting themselves even more.

I have brothers who seem to understand things only on the present level. Looking under things, at an unconscious level or deeper depth, is hard for them to see. The American people, or any people, need to get a sense of the complexity of human relationships. I think that is very important as it goes to the heart of our relationships. How can we be intimate if we don't understand all those things that are going on with the other person—or with society?

102

Mary's Story

Editor's Comments

The priest who raped Mary ordered her to go to another priest to hear her confession for a very good reason. Under canon law, various cardinals in the Vatican are in charge of different functions. One such office is the major penitentiary.

"The major penitentiary does not have a busy office. His work is extremely limited and mostly involves excommunications reserved to the Holy See. These are considered especially grave crimes. The excommunications reserved to the Holy See fall into five categories:

1. *For a bishop who consecrates a bishop without permission from the Holy See.*
2. *For desecration of the Eucharist.*
3. *For a priest breaking the confidentiality of a confession.*
4. *For a priest absolving his accomplice in a sexual sin.*
5. *For a person physically attacking the pope."*

This mean a priest, sexually abusing and raping a young girl, can go to confession for his sins and be granted absolution by the priest hearing his confession. Many predator priests have been reported by survivors to have done this, or at least said that they were going to confession.

The predator priest leaves the confessional in the state of grace, according to the Roman Catholic Church. His sexual abuse is considered a sin, not a crime.

Yet, if this same priest, after sexually abusing a young girl, were to hear her confession and grant her absolution, he would be eligible for excommunication. No wonder the priest ordered Mary to go to another priest to hear her confession.

It is also interesting to speculate on what sin the priest thought Mary was committing by being raped by a priest. And certainly, as a priest, he had to have known that one of the conditions of receiving absolution for a sin is to have a firm resolve to sin no more. As Mary says in her story, both of them knew it was going to happen again.

There is another aspect to this issue. Since the bishops and priests consider sexual abuse of children to be a sin, and not a crime, they apparently do not consider it necessary to report abusive priests to the civil authorities. In some cases, they have sent the abusive priests to treatment centers, but in far more cases they have simply reassigned the abusive priests to other parishes, without informing either parish of the accusations against the transferred priest.

This viewpoint that sexual abuse of children is a sin and not a crime has allowed many predator priests to molest and abuse children in many different parishes without fear of being reported to the local police.

It is also apparent that even today, in 2004, the authorities in the American Roman Catholic Church are determined to do whatever they can to continue to treat sexual abuse of children as a sin, outside of the United States criminal law system, and to be handled only by Church authorities.

It is quite apparent the sexual predator priests are not being controlled by the Church authorities.

I grew up in Cumberland, a small town in Western Maryland. I was the youngest of four kids in a very Catholic family. My parents were alcoholics. They both came from large, Catholic families, so there were always a lot of cousins, aunts, and uncles around our home. Maryland is a very Catholic state.

My three older siblings, two brothers and my sister Judy, were closer in age to each other than to me. They were all involved in sports together. My brothers played football and basketball, and Judy was a cheerleader. By the time I was a freshman, the next oldest sibling was a senior. So I wasn't very close to my brothers and sisters.

I worked as a secretary in the Saints Peter and Paul parish office my four years in high school. I was responsible for typing and filing, and each Monday I was given the collection from the Sunday masses to count and deposit in the bank. Working daily in the parish office gave the priests easy and direct access to me.

My cousin's grandfather abused me, but I think he abused many other females in the family. I never told anybody, because that was something you never did— tell somebody, I mean. It upset me terribly, and every time we visited I made every effort to keep from being alone with him.

The first priest abused me during my freshman or sophomore year in high school. He was Father Marius Elsener, and he is now deceased. Everybody in the parish loved him. His parishioners thought he was an absolutely wonderful man who could work miracles.

One day Father Marius asked me to go for a drive with him to check out the parish grounds where the annual parish picnic would be held. Like everyone in the parish, I looked up to Father Marius, and of course I was happy to take a ride with him.

He drove his car to the picnic area and we got out of the car. He walked me around the grounds for a few minutes. I didn't know what we were supposed to be doing or what we were supposed to be checking. Suddenly he stopped me and started touching me inappropriately.

I was mortified. I was terrified, with no idea what to do. Scared beyond belief. Even now, many years later, just thinking of that experience rekindles the emotions I felt then.

I didn't say anything to Father Marius. His touching didn't seem to go on long, but a minute is too long. Maybe thirty minutes or so. He didn't really have intercourse with me.

After he stopped, neither one of us said anything. I pretended like it never happened. Of course when I got home I didn't tell my parents.

Father Marius never approached me again, which confused me, but I was grateful. I was, however, horribly shamed by what had happened, thinking it must have been my fault at least partially.

About two years later, a new priest, Ronin Schreiber, came to the parish. He was my primary abuser.

Father Ronin had a very deep voice, which I can still hear today. He had a huge double chin. He wasn't fat, but very tall. And the Capuchins, the religious order at Saints Peter and Paul, wore long brown robes all the time. I had no idea why he selected me because there were other, prettier, girls at my high school. I am sure I was not his first, nor would I have been his last victim. I don't remember all the details of how it started, but most of what happened is crystal clear in my mind. He was my mother's age, close to fifty—not a young priest. This makes the abuse more disgusting.

Father Ronin first approached me one day in the parish hall. We had had basketball practice, and there were a bunch of girls in the hall. (I attended an all-girl Catholic high school—the parish was connected to the grade and high school, giving predators plenty of victims from which to choose). He took me aside, away from the other girls, and talked to me for a while. I don't remember what we talked about that first time, but, as he continued to befriend me, he talked about other people in the school. I remember once he told me that a girl, one year behind me in school, had been sent away because she was pregnant. I felt awkward knowing this, since it was none of my business. I never mentioned this to anyone else. Years later, I wondered if he had impregnated her.

Now, I understand this was just a ploy of his to develop a relationship with me. It meant we had a secret, just he and I, and I could not tell any of my friends about this secret. Soon I had other secrets about him that I could not discuss with my family or friends.

I never knew what to call him. He encouraged me to call him Greg; he said his birth name was Gregory. (Religious priests and nuns abandon their birth names when they join an order and take a different name; therefore his name "Ronin." I couldn't bring myself to call him Greg. He was, after all a PRIEST, a representative of God. How can you call someone in that position by a nickname—any name other than Father . . ."?

Anyway, he started getting personal with me—touching me when we were alone, talking with me. He told me he wanted to have intercourse with me.

I remember we met several times upstairs in the parish hall. This was a large building used for various parish functions. One end had a room upstairs used for the stage lights and sound system. There was an old dirty couch in that room, and that is where he eventually took my virginity.

I have difficulty remembering the details of the night he first had intercourse with me. It was not our first meeting; he had been preparing me for that night for some time. I do remember he always used a condom.

I didn't say anything to anyone. I was absolutely mortified and so confused. I felt I had no right to say no to anyone in authority. It was as if whatever he wanted to do with me was what he was going to do. If he had wanted to turn me into a prostitute, I am sure I would have gone along with that too.

This went on for well over a year. He would call me at home at night. This was stupid of him to do because he had a very recognizable voice. I don't know what my parents thought during this whole time. We never discussed it. We never talked about it. They died not knowing I had been abused. Ronin called me at least three times a week for more than one or maybe two years. I really don't know for sure, but it was a very long time.

When he called me, he would direct me to meet him at various places around the school and the church property. I don't think we ever met in the church itself, but he would have me meet him in the school a lot.

When he called, he would tell me which door to go to. He would meet me at the door, and of course he always carried a big bunch of keys that opened every door of the church and school. He would let me in, and then lock the door behind us. It was all very surreptitious. I was terrified all the time, because I was scared to death of what would happen if somebody saw me. I am not sure what I thought would happen to me for being in the school with a priest after hours, but the whole experience was terrifying to me.

Father Ronin would have sex with me in the classrooms, cloakrooms, the places where I had to go to school the next day. It was horrible for me. Horrible during the times he was abusing me. And horrible the next day when I would have to go to class in the same room where I had been raped the night before.

I remember one night when he told me to come up at a certain time. By the way, I lived within walking distance of the school, just two blocks away, so when he called I would walk up the hill to the school. I guess it didn't matter to him what the weather was like, since I would go up anyway.

I remember meeting him that night at the back of the hall. There was a doorway there. He had just come from a wedding rehearsal. For some reason, that stuck in my mind. The whole thing was abhorrent to me. He acted as if this was the way things were supposed to be. He took me into the room there and raped me.

One of the worst things about all of this was not just the experience, but what he told me I had to do. I asked him after the first time about going to communion. He told me I had to go to confession first, and he said he had to go to confession also.

This meant I couldn't go to communion during the week. I had to go to St. Patrick's Church every Saturday afternoon. I had to walk down there—some of the most humiliating times of my life. Because he told me that not only did I have to confess I was having sexual intercourse, but that I was having sexual intercourse with a priest. I didn't think about this then, but I have to wonder why the priests to whom I confessed each week didn't offer to help me. And what about the priest to whom he was confessing? The priests I was going to could so easily have offered to help me know what to do to stop this. This is clear proof of the enabling that has gone on in the Catholic Church for so long. During this time, I went to several different priests for my confession. None of them ever offered to help me. They just gave me my penance and sent me on my way. That was criminal on their part.

I was terrified one of the priests I went to for confession would find out who I was—which is why I had to go to a different parish for confession. The whole thing was so stupid because you cannot go to confession unless you promise God not to do it again. We both knew we were going to do it again. It was ridiculous.

One of the other things he did was just awful. Each Sunday when I went to mass, if he was saying the mass, he would try to give me two hosts to show how special I was to him. How disgusting.

In my senior year, I would go to school every day as if nothing was happening. It is a wonder how people survive these things, but somehow you do. At least, I did. It is like living a double life when you are sixteen years old.

The nun we had for our senior year home teacher was very nice and very kind. Sister Bernice. It is too bad I never confided in her. I probably could have, looking back, but I never told anybody about being abused. And who knows, she may have thought either I was lying to punish him for what she might have thought was an unrequited school girl crush. Or she may have kept quiet for the same reasons so many other religious people have over the years.

Eventually, and I am not real sure how I reached this decision, I decided I would go into the convent. It seemed the only option I had. To me, it was the only thing I could do so God would forgive me for what I had done.

— *Mary's Story*—

Until recently, anytime I would talk to a therapist I would say that I had had an affair with a priest. That is actually what I thought. I didn't think of it as sexual abuse. That is the absolute power priests have over so many people.

So naturally I thought I had to gain God's forgiveness. And to do that I decided to go into the convent, which, in many respects, was an odd decision for me to make.

My high school class was small, maybe thirty-two girls. There were three Catholic girls' high schools in Cumberland. There were, I think, two other girls in my class going into the convent. One stayed only two months; the other stayed for many, many years. While the other girls were preparing for college, I was preparing to go into the convent. I didn't think of this as the best thing for me to do; it was the only thing. This was the only way I could repent for what I had done. I could both repent and at the same time get myself out of the situation.

Father Ronin Schreiber told me that he was very glad I was entering the convent. I remember him telling me how glad he was, since that meant no other men would ever have me. And he thought that was just wonderful.

During my senior year, our teacher used to keep a large bottle of aspirin in her desk drawer. She had always told us that if we had a headache and needed an aspirin we could get one out of her desk.

One day, during the spring of my senior year, I started taking aspirin in the morning. By the end of the day I had taken the whole bottle. I was hoping I would die. Nobody noticed and nobody said anything. Nobody even noticed the aspirin bottle was empty. At the end of the day, I felt really light headed as I walked home.

When I arrived home I told my mother I wasn't feeling well, went up stairs to the bathroom and vomited. My mother, who had followed me upstairs and into the bathroom, looked at what I had thrown up. She said, "I wonder what it is. It looks like cottage cheese, but I know you don't eat cottage cheese." And that was the end of it.

I never told anyone I had tried to commit suicide. You probably can't kill yourself with aspirin, but I certainly didn't know that, and it was my intention to die to escape.

Finally, the day came and I entered the convent. I had been seeing Ronin every time he called, right up to the day I entered the convent in Louisville, Kentucky. This was a convent of the Ursuline Sisters, and was what they call a motherhouse.

I stayed in the convent for two and one half years before I had my nervous breakdown. Ronin visited me twice during my first year, which is called the postulate year. I wore a black uniform, but no habit. My classmates thought I was lucky to have a priest come down to visit and pay special attention to me. They didn't know what happened inside the visitors' room.

The first time Ronin visited me in the convent, I went into the visitors' room. I was wearing my little postulant uniform. Once again he molested me. I was terrified someone would come into the room, but I'm sure he knew they would never do that—not with a reverent priest visiting one of his former parishioners. I'm sure he felt perfectly safe.

That incident really disturbed me. I thought it could not be happening, but it was. It was like living in a parallel universe. I thought I would go to Hell for sure, for having sex with a priest in the convent. And I also realized at that time I wasn't safe from this predator even in the convent. As it turns out, I would not be safe from him until I was a patient in a psychiatric hospital in Louisville.

Father Ronin continued to visit me in my second and third years in the convent. I eventually started having what I learned later was a nervous breakdown. I slept no more than a few hours a night. I would leave my little room, our "cell" as they called it, and sit by the windowsill for hours most nights. My entire body was tied up in painful knots. I lost about forty pounds in a short period of time, and only weighed about 110 pounds to begin with.

The mother superior and other nuns noticed the change in my appearance. I had no idea what to say.

At that time, I honestly didn't know what was happening. I wasn't aware that it was all connected to the priest sexual abuse. Eventually they took me to a psychiatrist. After my second visit, they decided to recommend I enter Our Lady of Peace, a mental hospital in Louisville.

I was a patient there for two or three months. I believe the nuns in the convent wanted me in the hospital because it was their way of getting me out of the convent. I didn't know this at the time, and I don't know how much they knew about Father Ronin. But I was not someone they wanted in their convent.

Upon being admitted to the mental hospital, I was told I needed electric shock treatment. I had no medical training or information about this and no one to discuss this with. I knew nothing about the treatments and their aftereffects. But I was totally depressed and didn't care about anything. I was also heavily medicated. In fact, I remember one day not being able to walk without almost falling down—the medication was that strong.

The shock treatments were horrible. I remember waking up in the recovery room tied to a bed. I was terrified, and didn't know what was happening or where I was. I had six or eight sessions of shock treatment, receiving them every other day. On the in-between days I was so lethargic I couldn't do anything—even getting out of bed was a chore, but they forced me to get up.

116

And I was so doped up I couldn't do anything about what was going on.

There was one thing I was glad of. There is something about walking into a locked ward in a mental hospital. It was a relief to me, a little bit of a relief, because I thought I can do and say anything I want. It won't matter. Everyone here is crazy anyway. They don't expect anything of me. If I don't want to get up in the morning, I don't have to. If I don't want to eat, I don't have to. I don't even have to go into that stupid recreation room.

Eventually those shock treatments became part of my life. I became used to them, and they were just something I went through.

One other day is clear in my mind. A nurse came to tell me I had a visitor. My parents didn't live anywhere near, so I knew it would not be them. And then the nurse told me it was Father Ronin Schreiber. I looked at the nurse, and must have looked terrified. She told me I didn't have to have visitors if I didn't want to. I could tell him no.

It was the first time I had ever been able to tell him no. And I told the nurse I didn't want to see him. It felt good to tell him no. And I was aware that I was in a locked ward, and he could not get to me. I was safe, for the time being, from him. Locked up in a mental hospital.

When they finally decided to release me from the hospital, the mother superior and my class mother came to visit me. They told me they were kicking me out of the convent.

This made me really, really upset and angry with the mother superior. Just to be angry at the mother superior, and show it, took a lot of guts on my part. Of course I was full of drugs at the time. Anyway, my parents came down to pick me up and take me home.

My father had been an alcoholic all my life. I had been told that if he ever started drinking again it would kill him. Now there I was, leaving a mental hospital with no idea of what was going on in my life. On the way home, we had to stop one night in a motel since it was too long of a drive for one day. Once we were in the motel my mother told me my father had started drinking again. But only beer.

My immediate thought was my father was going to die. After the trauma I had just gone through, now I have to worry about my father drinking again. It was very bad timing on my mother's part, but I think she was doing the best she could.

I lived with my parents in Cumberland for some time, but I can't remember if this was days, weeks, or months. The electric shock treatments really effected my memory, and some of those memories I have never recovered.

No one in my family ever mentioned the mental hospital to me. Nobody ever asked me what it was like or why I was there. It was like it never happened. So I thought the entire family must be ashamed of me and I should leave town.

My sister was living in San Francisco. She came back to visit, and while she was there, it was somehow decided I would go live with her and get work out there. I think I lived with her and her roommates for six or eight months until I found my own roommate and moved into an apartment with her.

I was living a life with many secrets. I never told anyone about having an affair with a priest, as I still considered it. I never told anyone about having a nervous break-down and spending time in a mental hospital. When I filled out job applications I never mentioned any medical or mental problems.

The California Heart Association hired me as a secretary, working in their offices on Mission and Ninth Street in San Francisco. One day, during lunchtime, I was walking on Market Street, which is one block away from my office. I looked across the street and saw Father Ronin standing there. I almost died.

At the time I thought it was a coincidence. Now I know better. Nobody who comes to San Francisco as a tourist is standing on Market Street near Ninth Street. There is nothing Catholic there, and nothing to see. I know now he had found out where I worked and was stalking me. He didn't dare call me at my apartment, but somehow he found out where I worked.

I don't remember if I crossed the street over to him or if he crossed over to me. Anyway, we had a little bit of conversation there on the sidewalk. I still didn't think that what he had done to me was wrong; I still thought what I had done was wrong.

He asked me to dinner that night. I said yes.

After work that afternoon, I met him at some lounge in downtown San Francisco. I forget the name of the lounge, but it was near Union Square. I remember sitting in front of him and asking, "Don't you know what you did to me? Don't you know what happened to me? Do you know I ended up in a mental hospital after having a nervous breakdown?" I had a strong urge to scream at him, and tell him how badly he had hurt me. But I was brought up to act like a lady. We were in a nice place, and I had to act proper in public.

All during the evening I kept telling him, in different ways, how much he had hurt me. I wanted him to understand the devastation I had experienced from his actions.

Ronin did not seem to grasp what I was saying, or else he didn't care. He absolutely refused to admit he had done anything wrong. He told me my mental breakdown was not the result of his actions, but of some other things in my life.

Father Ronin ended up having sex with me that night. That is another horribly devastating part of this whole experience. After dinner and drinks we took a cab to my apartment. My roommate must have been out that night. When he left, I felt about as low and worthless as at any time in my life.

I had no one to talk to about this. I had to support myself, so I got up the next morning and went to work. I did my best to get through the period of depression that followed. I buried all thoughts and memories of this experience as quickly as I could. And as deeply as I could.

That one night reminded me just how big a hold Ronin had on me. He left, and that became another event in my life that I never mentioned to anyone.

I never heard from Father Ronin again. I never tried to communicate with him. One day my mother told me Ronin had developed cancer and died. He had died, but the influence he had on me stayed alive. It influenced my marriage, I am sure.

I met Dick, who was to become my husband, in March of 1968. He was twelve years older than I was. The fact that I was attracted to an older man is tied into my submissiveness to authority figures.

I was working for the public relations director for the California Heart Association. Dick had written a booklet titled "Introduction to EKG for Nurses." That was when the EKG equipment had first came out, and Dick had written an excellent book on the use of the EKG equipment. He told the Heart Association he would give them the rights to the booklet if they promised to give it away and not sell it.

The only sticking point was that Dick wanted to retain the copyright for the book in his name, and the association didn't agree. At least, not at first. It took a year until they finally agreed, and Dick received the credit he wanted. It was during this year that Dick asked me out for our first date. Three years later we married.

I have heard other victims of sexual abuse say you should never admit to anyone you were abused because it can come back to haunt you. It sure did for me, which means the victim has to continue to hold in silence all the pain and hurt they have suffered just to keep from being hurt again.

I can remember trying to talk to Dick once about this priest thing—and about my nervous breakdown. He had nothing to say about my time in the mental hospital. I guess people just don't know what to say about something like that. Certainly Dick did not understand how traumatic it was for me. He did have something to say about the priest. But not what I was looking for.

The priest sexual abuse happened in 1962 and 1963. I moved to San Francisco in May of 1966 and met Dick in 1968. We married later that same year. As I look back now, when I met Dick, the mental hospital and abuse had only occurred a few years earlier. When I told him about the abuse he responded, like many people do,

"That happened a long time ago. I don't know why you just don't forget it."

We had our first child, a son, in 1972, and our daughter was born in 1976. Dick was an excellent father and a good husband in spite of our problems and disagreements. But Dick was fighting his own personal demons. He attempted suicide twice unsuccessfully, first in 1982, then in February, 1984. The third time, March 9, 1984, he succeeded.

As a result of Dick's suicide I became a single mother of a seven-year-old daughter and an eleven-year-old son. Somehow we survived, but it meant I pushed the original abuse back into the recesses of my mind. And there it stayed for years.

One day in 2001, I read in the paper about the Oakland Diocese and the assistance they were providing to victims of sexual abuse by Catholic priests. I began by attending a meeting with other survivors. It was the first time I had spoken of the abuse except to counselors in the mental hospital and to my husband.

Most of the survivors I have met over the years reported their abuse, at some time, to family and authorities. I never did, and still haven't. I think however painful it is, it must be cathartic to tell your story to an audience. People need to know how horrible this is, and how far-reaching is its impact.

Mike's Story

Editor's Comments

Mike's story is the reason I decided to compile a book of survivors' stories. He is my younger brother, whose abuse took place in the late 1950s and early 1960s. Part of this time I lived at home, and for three years I was in the United States Army in Germany. I can still remember Father Cloutier driving up to our house on 15th Avenue in San Francisco and honking his car horn for Mike to come out and go for a ride with him.

Mike told me and his other brothers and sisters of the abuse one night in the mid-1990s. I am unsure of the exact year. We were having a family reunion at Brannan Island on the Sacramento River. It was late in the evening, perhaps 10:00 PM or so. We had more than forty of our family there, siblings, spouses, nephews, nieces, cousins, etc. There was a large bonfire, music, noisy kids, and a lot of eating and drinking. Most people were split up into smaller groups to talk or play games.

Mike and I were standing, just talking about something, and I don't remember how the topic of Cloutier came up. I do remember Mike telling me,

"I woke up around 2:00 AM and Cloutier has his hand on my penis."

I had no idea what I should do or say. I hugged Mike, told him I was sorry, and that ended the discussion as far as I was concerned. And I didn't pursue this subject until the late summer of 2002.

Reading the San Francisco Chronicle in August of 2002, I learned about the sexual abuse by Catholic priests in the Boston area, and how the abuse had been covered up and ignored by the bishops for decades. I started thinking it was the same way in San Francisco with the priest who had abused my brother. Cloutier had never been accused or charged with sexual misconduct that I knew of. He was still living his life as a respected Catholic priest, retired, but respected.

I called Mike and asked him two questions. First, did he believe a book on the subject of survivors of predator priests would be a worthwhile book? He answered yes.

My second question was harder for him to answer. I asked if he would give me his story for publication. He thought about that for a few seconds and replied yes. That took a lot of courage for Mike to agree to go public with his story of being abused since he had never spoken about it openly before.

As we spoke, during that initial conversation and later ones as well, we discussed what our father, who died in 1971, would have done if Mike had told him he was being sexually abused by a Catholic priest. We agreed that our father would probably not have believed Mike.

Our father was a devout, practicing Catholic who attended mass daily at Saint Patrick's in downtown San Francisco and Sunday mass at Star of the Sea. I do not believe he would have been able to accept the idea that the priest who heard his confession, gave him Holy Communion, and was his conduit to God, was abusing his son. Believing this would have required him to totally rethink his life and his devotion to the Catholic Church.

This is not an uncommon theme in the survivors' stories. For example, Jennifer's mother, in spite of the fact that her husband was the grand knight of the Knights of Columbus, wondered if the parish would believe her if she said the monsignor was sexually molesting her daughter.

This refusal on the part of parishioners to believe one of "their" priests could be guilty of sexually abusing a child continues to this day.

The center of our family life was Star of the Sea, the Roman Catholic Church located at 8th Avenue and Geary Street in San Francisco. My parents were both happy and proud when I became an altar boy. I was following in the steps of my two older brothers, both of whom had been altar boys for many years. And my two younger brothers followed in my footsteps. Later Johnny (son number four) attended St. Patrick's Seminary in Menlo Park for four years. Long after I was sexually molested by Father Cloutier, a parish priest at Star of the Sea. Cloutier was one of, if not the biggest and best, fund raisers the Catholic Church had in the entire San Francisco Bay Area.

My whole family attended mass at Star of the Sea, following a family tradition that we all attend mass together every Sunday. That had been true in North Dakota and Montana, where we had lived before my father was transferred by the US Army Corps of Engineers to their San Francisco office in 1955.

By the time we bought a house at 15th and Lake Street, in the Richmond district, my older brothers and sister were "too old" to attend mass with the family. Of course, they were still expected to attend mass every Sunday and receive Communion, even if they did not attend with the family.

My father had several options for his next assignment when the work in Riverdale, North Dakota, on the Garrison Dam, was ending. Both he and my mother chose San Francisco. They thought it would be the best city to ensure their eight children could receive a Catholic education and then go to a Catholic college. On more than one occasion, my mother told me that they selected San Francisco so that Ed, the oldest son, could go to the University of San Francisco, a Jesuit run university.

All eight Handlin children did receive a Catholic education. In 1956, when I was eleven years old, the oldest seven kids were all in Catholic schools. My two older brothers attended Sacred Heart High School. My older sister, next younger brother, my two younger sisters, and I attended Star of the Sea Grammar School. When my youngest brother was old enough, he also attended Star of the Sea Grammar School. When the boys graduated from the eighth grade, they had a choice of Sacred Heart, St. Ignatius, or Riordan High Schools. It was understood the girls would attend Star of the Sea Girls High School. For twelve years, there was a Handlin daughter at Star of the Sea Girls High School.

We were a very Catholic family. The teachings of the Church were the guidelines for our entire family life. For example, during Lent we said the Rosary at the dinner table every night.

It was also when I was eleven that Father Cloutier first molested me. At least, that is the first time I can remember. It happened one night at Santa Cruz. Father Cloutier had taken two of us, Jake (not his real name) and myself, for a weekend in Santa Cruz. We drove down to Santa Cruz on a Saturday. We spent the day riding the big roller coaster and having a great time. Then we checked into a motel for the night. This was the third or fourth time the three of us had gone to Santa Cruz for the weekend. After dinner, Father Cloutier would give us a sleeping pill so we would get a good night's sleep. At least, that is what he told us. I don't know if Jake took his pill or not, but I did.

I woke up at 2:00 in the morning when I became aware that Father Cloutier had his hand around my penis. Jake and I were sharing one of the twin beds in the motel room, as we usually did. I remember wishing Jake would wake up, because he would know what to do. Then I realized Jake was awake and participating in this. I didn't know what to do, so I pretended to be asleep. It was the scariest experience I have ever had.

I realized Father Cloutier and Jake both had their hands on my penis. They proceeded to masturbate me. I don't remember if I reached an orgasm or not. I probably was still too young, but I can still recall both of them playing with my penis. I was scared to death.

Then the two of them went off on their own, to the other side of the bed or to the other twin bed in the room. The details of this are fuzzy. What I do remember about that first time was being so terribly scared. We had had such a great time at the Boardwalk that day. I think I rode the roller coaster more than twenty times. Now I lay in bed being molested by a man I believed was the right hand of God.

This sexual abuse during trips with Father Cloutier continued to happen for a long time, for many years. Father Cloutier would invite me out, and I felt powerless to say no. What could I tell my parents? How would I explain why I did not want to go some place with Father Cloutier, one of God's chosen few? I couldn't. My parents were so happy and proud that a

Catholic priest was inviting one of their sons for weekend trips that there was no way I could decline the invitations. I am not even sure my parents would have believed my story if I could have told them what Cloutier did to me on these weekend trips. And so Cloutier continued to stop by our house, honk his horn, and I would go out and get in his car.

The trips to Santa Cruz and elsewhere in California happened countless times. On many occasions, there would be two or three of us young boys, all from Star of the Sea Grammar School. We would do something in the day that was fun and that we could tell our parents about, then check into a motel.

Father Cloutier would give us sleeping pills before we went to bed to be sure that we would sleep all night. But if he forgot the sleeping pills, he would give us Scotch to drink. I was probably about twelve or thirteen when he gave me a drink of Scotch for the first time. As we got older, he encouraged us to drink more Scotch. He was an evil man—an evil, evil man.

Typically during these weekends we would check into a motel, go out for dinner and then go back to the motel and watch a little TV until it was bedtime. The motel rooms always had two double beds. Jake and I would share one bed while Cloutier would sleep in the other.

A few minutes after lights, out Cloutier would sneak into our bed and start fondling us. After he discovered I was awake and aware of what he was doing, he no longer kept up the pretense of "sleep" but would get into our bed and start playing his games. If Jake was being uncooperative, he would take his belt and whip Jake while I watched. Whipping always got Cloutier very excited. Although he could not maintain an erection, it was obvious he really enjoyed whipping Jake.

I didn't know how to get out of it. I couldn't tell my parents. I couldn't tell any other priests. And I certainly couldn't tell any of my friends. I remember thinking as a teenager that, if anyone found out, I would kill myself—commit suicide. I am convinced today that I would have if anyone ever discovered what was going on. I was literally scared to death to say no to Father Cloutier.

I was afraid of Father Durkin, another parish priest at Star of the Sea. He was a giant of a man with a powerful presence. I was afraid to approach him. There was no one I could turn to.

Telling the pastor, Monsignor Fleming, or Father Durkin was not an option. I believed that, had I told them about Cloutier, they might have molested me themselves and covered up my story. They certainly would not have helped me. Father Cloutier molested me in his suite in the church rectory while other priests were in the rectory. They had to suspect something yet did nothing.

Looking back, I did not have any evidence at that time to support my belief that Monsignor Fleming and

Father Durkin would have molested me had I approached them about Father Cloutier. I just felt they must have known about Cloutier molesting me and did nothing. So I was afraid to approach them.

We took some great trips. We went to Phoenix a couple of times. We went to LA regularly, and Father Cloutier would knock on movie stars' doors and line them up for a church festival. In the fifties and early sixties, Father Cloutier raised $60,000 with a weekend festival at Star of the Sea. That was very impressive. He was celebrated as a fund raiser.

Father Cloutier was a great salesman. He would knock on a star's front door and ask them to appear at the festival. "Harvest Jubilee" was the name of the festival at Star of the Sea. Dennis Day was a good Irish Catholic and appeared seven years in a row. I swam in Dennis Day's swimming pool with his kids (he had a bunch) on one of our visits.

We had a soft drink in Barbara Whiting's apartment while Cloutier and the Whiting Sisters discussed their upcoming appearance. Father Cloutier was adept at using his Roman collar to induce these big stars into appearing. He would play on the stars' success and their obligation to help the Church.

One time, Father Cloutier knocked on Liberace's front door. Liberace apologized for not being able to attend the Star of the Sea Festival, but insisted we use his car and driver. And we did. For an entire week, we rode around in Liberace's limo with Liberace's chauffeur.

During our trips to Los Angeles, Father Clothier introduced me to several important people. They were generous friends of his. One such friend was Roy Smith. I believe Roy Smith was the president of Cal Tech Industries. He invented Handy Andy and later sold the rights for this product to Lever Brothers. He was a big, powerful salesman type. He had a big house in the hills of Hollywood or Santa Monica. The house had a 360 degree view of the mountains and the ocean. It was magnificent.

When we flew down to LA, Roy Smith would pick us up at the airport. He always offered Father Cloutier one of his cars, either a brand new Cadillac or a brand new T-Bird—brand new because he bought a new one of each year. We stayed at the same hotel every visit. I think it was called the Sahara, but I am not sure. Roy Smith always told the hotel to send him the bill.

He was impressed with Father Cloutier. Roy Smith was on his second marriage, and Father Cloutier told him it was OK to participate in the sacraments. In exchange for this dispensation, I think he gave Father Cloutier a lot of money. He would take us out to some fancy restaurants. It was all impressive and heady to a thirteen year old boy.

I had heard rumors when I was in the eighth grade, when I was about twelve or thirteen years old, that

Father Cloutier would tell people who were dying that if they left their house to the Church they would see Heaven. These were just rumors, told to me by other classmates, but to be honest I never doubted that the rumors could be true. Cloutier had no morals and would tell anyone anything if it would further his cause.

Father Cloutier was so good at fund raising that, when I was about fifteen or sixteen, he was transferred to Corpus Christi Parish in Oakland. He had one dinner there and raised half a million dollars. That was a lot of money in 1960. He was transferred because the pastor at Corpus Christi had several million dollars in the bank, but let the bishop know he was not going to use any of his money to remodel the church, the school, and the convent. The facilities were badly in need of repair and renovation. So the Church transferred Father Cloutier to Corpus Christi, and he did the necessary fund raising.

Since Father Cloutier was so successful at raising funds for Corpus Christi, he was transferred to St. Rose in Pleasanton to do the same thing. St. Rose was a small parish with a small church, but the bishop knew St. Rose was in a growing area. He told Father Cloutier to build a large church, school, and gym. Someday soon the whole valley would be covered with engineers and their families. Cloutier raised the funds and built the new facilities. He was very successful.

While Father Cloutier was at Star of the Sea, his sexual abuse of me went on at least weekly. Father Cloutier would call me and tell me that he was coming by my house. He would drive up in front of our house and honk the horn. I would go out, and he would let me drive around in Golden Gate Park. I was only fourteen years old, so that was special to me. While I drove, he would play with my penis and masturbate himself. But I could drive his car. Sometimes after driving around the park, we would get a motel room out on the beach. He would molest me there.

We went to Santa Rosa quite regularly for weekends. That allowed him to go to confession on Sunday morning after molesting me Saturday night. He would go to confession to a priest there that I think was one of the priests who participated in this. I believe there was a whole ring of priests who helped each other with the child abuse they all participated in. In any case, Cloutier always went to the same church and, I think, to the same priest for his confession. Then Father Cloutier would feel he was in good grace again and could return to Star of the Sea and say mass.

Before Father Cloutier left Star of the Sea, he would take me to his room at the rectory, his suite really, and molest me there while other priests were also in the rectory. I have no doubt that the other priests knew what was going on. Particularly Monsignor Fleming. I had dinner a number of times with Father Cloutier in the rectory, several times when other priests were present.

There were never any other boys or girls. I have often wondered what the housekeepers thought when the priest had a young boy for a dinner guest and then spent time in his room alone with the boy.

Father Cloutier gave me a car when I was seventeen years old, just before he was transferred to Oakland. This enabled me to drive to where he was so he wouldn't have to come and pick me up. He also gave me money from the time I was about fourteen years old.

While at St. Rose in Pleasanton, Cloutier obtained several porno films that he would show me while he fondled me and orally copulated me. These films usually showed women being beaten and abused. Afterwards he would give me twenty dollars and send me home. Many times I thought of myself as a prostitute.

This went on until I was about nineteen or twenty, and my girlfriend became pregnant. When my girlfriend told me she was pregnant, I took her to see Father Cloutier at St. Rose in Pleasanton. I knew he would tell her not to marry me. He would tell her I was too immature. And Father Cloutier did not suggest we get married. Instead he told my girlfriend to either have an abortion or move into St. Anne's Home for Unwed Mothers. My girlfriend cried all the way back to San Francisco from Pleasanton.

I drove back to San Francisco. All the way home I listened to her cry. I didn't want her to have an abortion, and I couldn't just walk away from what would become my child. We decided to get married.

Father Cloutier continued to call me after my marriage. I think I saw him two more times after I was married. Then I got up the courage to say no. And I have never seen him since. He telephoned me several years ago and asked me for money. I didn't respond.

During the years I was molested, it never occurred to me to report Cloutier to a bishop. I never believed a bishop would support me or believe my story against the word of a priest. It was not until years later, when my wife suggested I talk with a priest about this sexual abuse, that I decided to discuss this with a priest. I picked Father Brian Joyce. My wife and I had attended mass at his church and listened to his sermons. I respected his thinking and his philosophy.

When I told my story to Father Brian Joyce at Corpus Christi Church in Oakland, it was a relief of some sorts. Hardly a day in my life has gone by that I have not thought of Cloutier. Here was a chance for me to tell someone who might be able to do something about it. I never mentioned any names, but he knew whom I was talking about within five minutes of my telling him my story.

Father Joyce was a real revelation to me. He told me I was the one who had been sinned against. He acknowledged it must be difficult for me to go to church—which is very true. He told me he knew who I was talking

138

about and later told me that he had never liked or respected Cloutier.

A few months later, Father Joyce called me and said he needed to see me. When I got to the church, he told me that a story was going to break in the San Francisco Chronicle naming Monsignor Durkin, Monsignor Heaney, Monsignor Armstrong and several other priests I knew from my childhood as being accused of abuse. He wanted me to find out from him rather than read the paper and discover it.

These priests are all men I respected and looked up to. I was taught priests are right next to God and are all powerful. For example, on my first day in the seventh grade I sat at a desk that had the word F_ _K carved in it in letters about two or three inches in height. I thought it was funny. I showed all my boy classmates and they agreed it was funny.

About six weeks into the school year, Sister Florentine discovered the carving and sent me to the principal's office. The principal, Sister Donate Marie, suspended me from school as I would not admit to carving it.

I was sent home early to tell my mom. My mom was upset with me. The next day Father Durkin asked why I wasn't in school. Upon finding out that I had been suspended, he told the principal, "If Michael said he didn't do it, he didn't do it. I want him back in school now!" What power a priest had! I was allowed back in school the next day.

Something similar happened with the police when I was in high school and wrongfully accused of causing trouble. Father Durkin came to my rescue and told the police to leave me alone. A priest even had power over the police! WOW!

The abuse by Cloutier ended when I finally told him no. The pain and suffering caused by his abuse did not end. It still hasn't. Yet I think there are some lessons that can be learned from my experience.

I have learned I am stronger than I thought. But I am also very vulnerable to authority. I have also learned that, with time and the right help, I can overcome this trauma. I have also learned there is no way to correct these wrongs. This has affected my life and the lives of many of those close to me over the years, especially the three children born to my first wife. My firstborn child, my only son, and I are estranged. I think it is a direct result of the betrayal and abuse I received from Cloutier. There is no closure to this nasty experience. I can only hope to learn to live with it.

Telling my story has helped me start my healing process. Part of this was because when I did tell my story, I was introduced to a therapist. She is the first counselor who truly understands my pain and can actually help me through this healing process. I know my childhood was lost, my ability to have normal relationships without anxiety was lost, my ability to trust people in a relationship was lost, my ability to love myself and to trust myself was lost. I will never be able to regain these things.

I hope by my telling this story of abuse by Cloutier, people will understand just how evil he is and how much pain he caused—not just the pain to me and the other survivors he abused, but the pain he caused to our families and friends.

It is not easy to tell a story of abuse by a priest. I told my first wife after seven or eight years of marriage. I told my second and third wives prior to our marriage. But, when I tried to tell a friend, when I was in my early twenties, he did not understand. He ridiculed victims. I was afraid to say anything more to him, or to anyone else either. I feared someone else might have the same reaction.

When I told my sisters and brothers several years ago, after a lot of publicity of clergy abuse had come out in the papers, they all were helpful and supportive. But it took that long, more than thirty years, for me to talk about this abuse with anyone except a therapist.

For myself, I hope to gain some peace in my life. I want to be able to sleep without nightmares. I want a day without anxiety. I want to feel that I am an okay person.

And the biggest hope I have, and the greatest reason for telling my story, is to prevent this type of abuse from happening to my children, or my grandchildren, or any other children. I have a daughter the same age now as I was when the abuse started. I shudder to think of someone so young and innocent being abused the way I was.

Sharan's Story

Editor's Comments

Sharan, as a young girl, was taught that the police were her friends and she could rely on them. Yet the one time, during her abuse by Father Victor Ortino, when the police became aware of her sexual abuse, they did not assist her. Sadly, this is a common theme for many of the survivors.

Priests, and especially bishops, enjoy a position of respect and prestige in their local communities. Many priests work with the local law enforcement agencies, including the police, on issues dealing with crime, child welfare, drug abuse, etc. Some priests function as a chaplain to Catholic and other police officers, particularly when a police officer is wounded or killed in the line of duty. As such, they become well known and respected by the individual police officers.

This respect given by the police officers to priests, even those suspected of being child molesters, when the child molesters are Catholic priests, was illustrated in San Francisco, California, in February, 2003. Monsignor John Heaney, seventy-five years old, had been charged with eight felony counts of molest-

ing a boy for more than two years, starting in 1961 when the child was seven years old.

At a bail hearing for Monsignor Heaney, a deputy chief of the San Francisco Police Department and dozens of police officers appeared in court in an apparent show of support. During this bail hearing, Heaney's bail was reduced from $800,000 to $150,000.

Survivor advocates were outraged by this apparent show of support for an accused child molester, believing it sent the wrong message to other survivors.

Of particular concern to the survivors was the show of support by police officers, some in uniform. As they noted, the police should be non-biased guardians of the law.

My mother was a fanatical Catholic. My father was a Catholic too, but not fanatical like my mother. My mother would go to weekday mass every morning, and of course take me with her. I can recall going with her when I was about seven years old. At that time, we were in St. Villamina's parish in Cleveland, Ohio, where I was born.

I attended the parish grammar school at St. Villamina's for the first three grades. I liked being in school and enjoyed being with the other kids. But sometimes, at recess, I would go into the church and talk to Jesus—talk to him just like he was there with me. Not every day, but sometimes I wanted to talk with Jesus more than I wanted to play with the other kids in my class. That was the kind of Catholic background I grew up in.

When I was nine years old, we moved to Painsville, Ohio and bought a house, our first house. My father worked for Greyhound as a bus driver. When we moved to Painsville, he started his own driving school, but continued to work for Greyhound. My father liked driving, and taught me to drive when I was nine. He taught me how to tune up a car when I was eleven. He had a great sense of humor and was fun to be around.

I was close to my dad and not close at all to my mother. I ran to see my father when he came home from work every evening. My mother was a good caretaker, but she was not a nurturer. A lot of that had to do with the way she was raised. She once told me that her mother, my grandmother, believed and lived this way. In raising children, when they became old enough to walk, you stopped hugging them.

This meant my mother didn't get a lot of affection when she was growing up, and as a result she was not an affectionate mother. She was very distant, emotionally, from her children. I don't think she connected with any of us. But my dad and I connected really well. In fact, when I look back on our family situation, I think my mother resented my closeness with my father. This probably served to widen the gap between us.

In terms of sexual information or education, I received nothing from my mother or my father. A few weeks before my twelfth birthday, right before Christmas, my period started, and I didn't know what it was, or what was happening. I thought I was bleeding to death. I was terrified. I thought I was dying. I sat on the toilet, bleeding, for at least five minutes, maybe a lot longer, before I called my mother. I was absolutely terrified. Her response was to put her arms around me and hug me. She told me I was not her little girl anymore.

That was it. She did tell me this will happen every month. But she didn't tell me why. She didn't tell me what was going on in my body to cause this. She just told me it was OK, trying to calm me down. I was crying and upset.

That was the extent of my sexual education by my mother. I am talking about for my entire childhood.

Once my dad said the "F___" word when my parents were fighting. I was a teenager at that point, it was after Father Ortino had started raping me, but I still didn't know what it meant. I had never heard it before. I was nineteen when I found out what the "F___" word meant.

Painsville was a small town of about 18,000 population. I never knew anyone in Painsville who was divorced. You didn't hear about anyone getting divorced. It was a very repressed community, although maybe that is not the correct word. The social life was very conservative. Nobody ever did anything out of the ordinary. You could walk from one end of the town to the other and pass people you had never seen and both of you would smile and say hello. That was the kind of town it was. Very friendly on the outside, but repressed on the inside.

My mother was always concerned about what the neighbors would think. That was a major concern for her, I recall. This had a major impact on how she lived her life and how her children lived their lives. My twin sisters were born when I was fourteen. When I was sixteen, another set of twin sisters were born. Both sets of twins were unplanned pregnancies. My parents relied on the rhythm method for birth control. Being Catholic, they could not use any contraceptives to avoid pregnancies.

I was in the eighth grade in St. Mary's grammar school. I was happy and doing well in my life. I had been a tomboy growing up, which helped me to be physically active in all the girls' sports. I had been playing baseball with the boys for several years; playing girls' sports was easy.

I had an exuberance for life. I was having fun and doing OK in school. Not great, but once in a while I received an A to go with the rest of my grades, which were mostly B's and C's. Then Victor Ortino arrived. My life changed from that day on.

The day Father Ortino came to Painsville, he rode in on my father's bus—technically, the Greyhound bus my father drove that day. My father came home that evening and told us we had a new priest in the parish. I am not sure exactly when Father Ortino arrived, perhaps January of 1950.

The reason I remember the date is that in September of 1950, St. Mary's decided to have a ninth-grade class, with different teachers for each subject. They were trying to find a way to develop a Catholic high school in the community. I was in the ninth grade that year, and Ortino became our Latin teacher.

When St. Mary's added the ninth grade to their grammar school, they also added a ninth grade girls' basketball team. This was the first time St Mary's had ever had a girls' team, and I was excited about being on the team. We had regular practice twice a week. Soon after we started, Father Ortino became involved with the team. He drove us home from practice, he drove us to and from the games, so we were seeing a lot of him.

I remember the beginning of school, when Father Ortino was our Latin teacher. One of the first things he did was to call my name and the name of another Italian girl in the class, Theresa Viochittee. He had us stand up. So the two of us stood up. That was it, and then he told us to sit down.

My great grandfather came over from Italy. His last name was Falotico, which is the same spelling that I use now. His son, my grandfather, was in vaudeville. In order to fit his name on the marquee, he had to shorten it, to Flatico. So he went by that name, and that was the name on my father's birth certificate. I was born with that name, or that spelling, on my birth certificate. About fifteen years ago, I changed the spelling of my last name, as did one of my sisters, to the original spelling. I think some of the changing had to do with being authentic in terms of my family history, but also in getting away from who I was at thirteen, to get away from being Sharon Flatico. I had earlier changed my name to Sharan when I was in India in 1992. Sharan means surrender of the ego, and I thought that was as good a name as anything.

Father Ortino would always drive me home last after practice or games. It didn't seem unusual since I lived the farthest away from town. He would tell me to sit next to him. There were six or seven of us kids in his car, and we would just pile in. He always wanted me to sit next to him. This went on for at least a month.

One night, after he had dropped off all the other girls, he asked me if I wanted to drive his car. He had a brand new blue Mercury. I had never driven a new car. I was all excited at the thought of driving his new car. "Yes," I told him.

He told me we would have to go out of town since he didn't want us to get caught. I didn't have a driver's license since I was only thirteen. I was not old enough to even have a learner's permit.

Even without a driver's license I drove my father's car. We lived a block away from a rural road, and the general store was a mile down this road. My father would let me drive to the store myself, which was kind of risky since I was only thirteen. But we never saw police officers out our way. I guess my dad was not very law abiding either, when I look back at that.

Ortino drove me out to a dirt road outside of the town area. I remember the dirt road vividly. I think he got out of the car on the driver's side and told me to slide over. I did not get out of the car. I slid over, and he walked around and got in the passenger side, where I had been sitting. I remember I was holding the steering wheel with both hands. I could see through the steering wheel, even though I was not tall enough to see over the wheel. I could see the dirt road in front of the car. The car headlights were on, but I can't remember if the engine was running or not. On both sides of the road there was nothing. No houses in sight on either side. It was a deserted, rural road—a deserted dirt road, no less.

I have since had body work on my left shoulder. Once, when the body worker was working on my left shoulder, I had this exact vision. It was just like being back on that rural dirt road with Ortino. The room where I was having the body work done was open to the outside, and I could see the trees just outside of the room. I felt the same sense of terror and panic I had felt in that car with Ortino the first time.

I yelled at the body worker to shut the door. The view out of that door was triggering the same emotions I had felt the first time I was raped. I was reliving that moment. There was something in my left shoulder that had locked that memory into my body cells.

I was sitting behind the steering wheel, excited at the prospect of driving a new car. Ortino leaned over toward me from the passenger seat. I remember I was looking at the dials on the dash board, and it looked like the instrument panel of an airplane. I wanted to know what all of the gauges and dials meant, and I thought he was leaning over to explain them to me. And he started to kiss my check and my neck.

I just gripped the steering wheel. I was looking straight ahead, saying, "Please don't. Please don't." I was terrified. I was whispering the words. I didn't know what to do. I know there were a few moments where the thought went through my mind to jump out of the car and run.

There was snow on the ground. Not on the dirt road, but on the ground on either side of the road, by the barren trees, which went on and on into the distance. I thought, for a moment of jumping out and running—just running anywhere.

There was something so bizarre, so wrong about what he was doing. Beyond that point, I cannot recall anything that went on that night. I have gone through hypnosis and everything anyone could think of to bring that memory back. I cannot recall what happened at all.

Subsequent to that, I remember every single time it went on. He would always tell me to get in the back seat. I would get in the back seat, obedient little Catholic girl that I was. I would sit there very stiff on the edge of the back seat, just dreading what was going to happen. He would then get into the back seat and push me down into the corner of the seat, where the end of the seat met the door of the car. My neck was bent, because I didn't sit. I couldn't put my head down flat, not the way he pushed me into position.

He had me so my legs were half off the seat. I would be there with my legs together. I was stiff, rigid—absolutely rigid. And every single time, I thought to myself that he would not do this again. He will see that I didn't want to do this, and he will stop. I would hold my legs so rigid and tight together that he would have to pry my legs apart.

He would tell me to take my panties down and I wouldn't. I wouldn't say anything, but I didn't take my panties down. He would have to pull them down with my legs rigidly together. I mean, this was a struggle for him every single time. It was like a ritual. Another Catholic ritual. Finally he would get my panties down.

And then he would pull my legs apart. Force them apart, because I was rigid. A body worker once told me that she had worked on thousands of women over the years. She has found that women who have thighs, called saddle bag thighs, everyone she has ever worked on who has them was molested as a child. She thought that was incredibly interesting. It must be something about the musculature and the reaction to the abuse like I went through that gets stored in the body.

He never took off my blouse. He never touched my breasts or anything. He never kissed me on the lips. Except for the first time when he kissed me on the neck and check, he never kissed or touched me again. He never took any of my clothing off except my panties.

First of all, it was winter. The back seat of his car was not a warm place. It was not just uncomfortable. It was freezing. I was freezing. I hate being cold. To this day, if I get cold, I get angry. I immediately get angry. I can't get cold. I can't tolerate it.

Father Ortino would remove his pants and underwear. He pushed them down; I don't think he took them all the way off. But I remember one time the police caught him. One time. He was on top of me. They shined their flashlights into the backseat of the car while he was on top of me. I know that time he must have taken his pants off. But he would still have his coat on. And that Catholic shirt kind of thing. But you know, I can't remember if he wore a Roman collar or not. I can't remember.

When the cops shined their flashlights on him they told him to get out of the car. I was terrified and I was relieved. I was thinking, "Thank God, Thank God." Because there was no denying what he was doing. He was on top of me. When he got out of the car he still had his shoes on. He always left his shoes on. I heard the cops tell him, in a very disgusted tone, "Get your pants on. Get back in the car and get your pants on."

He got back in the car and put his pants on. Then he got out of the car again and walked over to talk with the cops. For a long time he talked to the cops. For a very long time.

At one point, one of the cops came over to the car and shone his light on me. I was sitting with my head down. Just sitting on the back seat with my head down. I wish I would have had the sense at that time to just look up and say "Help me." Even to mouth the words. I was sure they were going to stop it. I was positive. There was no way they were not going to stop it. No question in my mind. But they didn't.

And then when Ortino was getting back into the car, one of the cops yelled at him, "Don't let us catch you back here again." And they left. I was absolutely broken. I couldn't believe they had left.

In fact, I have gone back to the current chief of police in Painsville and tried to find out how I could contact those guys because I want to find out what they remember about that night and what were they thinking—not to hurt them, but to let them know the pain this caused and tell them they could have done something to stop that pain. I have no idea what Ortino said to the police that caused them to get in their car and leave.

The chief of police, who has been very helpful to me, has made all kinds of excuses. I filed a police report with him this last summer, the summer of 2002. I asked him to at least contact retired cops and give them my phone number and ask them to call me. I don't have to have their phone numbers, or even their names. But he said he couldn't find them. I can't believe that. Not for a police department. How can they not have records? They have to be available, somewhere.

I know I am going back fifty years, so they would be in their eighties or even dead. And I said that to the police chief. But who knows, maybe they are still alive, or maybe they said something to somebody— maybe someone in their family, or to a fellow police officer who is still alive.

Ortino had trouble getting and maintaining an erection. I would say in the five months that he abused me he was able to penetrate me no more than three times. I remember it was a five month period, and it was one, two, or three times a week. Mostly it was twice a week, but once in a while one or even three times, usually twice. When he couldn't get an erection, which was usually the case, he just kind of bounced up and down on me with his fat belly.

Now, as an adult, I think he was pathetic. My neck was hurting, and I was afraid to tell him and wanting him to stop; and all this time, he would be bouncing up and down and not even close to my vagina—just bouncing on top of me. It was weird.

I don't remember him groaning or moaning, not the few times he ejaculated. He would always be holding his penis with his fingers. He always pulled out before he ejaculated. I found out many years later, from Father McMahon, that Ortino had molested a girl in Philadelphia. When I heard that, I wondered if he had made that girl pregnant. Maybe that was why he was so afraid of ejaculating even near my vagina.

The abuse from Ortino ended when Father McMahon, my rescuer priest, found out I was being sexually abused by his fellow priest. I had stopped going to daily communion, although I still went to mass every morning. By the way, two weeks after it started, the bus driver who drove us to school every day asked me "What is wrong?" He asked me what was wrong because I had changed so much in two weeks. I was frightened that he might have seen something was wrong with me. I just said nothing. I had changed so much. God, how I had changed.

Anyway, Father McMahon saw I wasn't going to communion, and he stopped me in the hallway and asked me about it. I just said, "I don't know," but I kept my head down while he was talking to me. I didn't say anything. He let me walk away that time.

Then one evening, as I was walking through the school yard on my way home, and nobody else was around, Father McMahon saw me. He called me over, and I walked over to him.

I just stood there, with my head down, not looking at him. He asked me "Why don't I see you at communion anymore?" I don't know what I said, but I would not look at him. He reached over and put his fingers on my chin and raised my head up so he could see my face. But I averted my eyes, I would not look at him. Then he let me go.

The next morning, right before Latin class, Father McMahon sent someone over to the class to summon me to the rectory. He was going to talk to me while Ortino was busy in the Latin class, teaching. So I would know I was safe, I guess.

He called me into the rectory. I sat in a chair, with my head down, not talking. He said to me, "Father Ortino is driving you home from basketball games." It was not a question, it was a statement.

Then he asked me, "Is Father Ortino driving you home last?"

I didn't answer him, nor did I speak to him, I just kept my head down. He told me to shake my head for yes or no, since I wouldn't speak to him. I kept my head down, but shook my head yes or no to his questions.

I think he went through a list of questions. I don't remember the exact wording.

Finally he got to the issue of sexuality. I don't remember how he phrased his question, but I shook my head yes. He let out a sound like an inhuman bellow. I had never heard anything like it in my life. Not before, and not since. It was inhuman, like an animal in pain. Then he cursed.

I was shocked at the curse. I don't remember what it was, but I was shocked. It might have been "Son of a Bitch!" or something like that. But I was shocked, because I didn't hear that kind of language. Not from anybody. And from a priest? Here this other priest can be doing what he is doing to me, but I was shocked when Father McMahon cursed? It was bizarre.

I remember my head just flew up, because I was so shocked he had cursed. Father McMahon told me that day, the day he found out, that I didn't have to do that anymore. I felt such relief upon hearing those words.

Within a day or two, the pastor, Monsignor Golina, called me in and asked me about it. I just shook my head yes to his questions. Monsignor Golina was a very old man, and he mumbled a lot. He sounded a lot like the pope does today. I didn't know what he was saying, or if he was praying or what.

Within a very short time, Father McMahon told me that Ortino would be leaving in a few days. Monsignor Golina had reported him to the diocese, and his abuse of me ended. I guess they confronted Ortino about this. I am sure they did.

Father McMahon also told me I didn't have to tell my parents. He said it just like that. He didn't tell me not to tell my parents; he told me I didn't have to tell my parents. He told me that Monsignor Golina and he would not tell my parents. That made me in collusion with them. They were going to help me keep it hidden. It was almost as if it was my fault, but the priests were going to help me hide it. The unspoken message that came through from that stayed with me for years.

The shame, guilt, and humiliation was there. It was just there. Father McMahon told me I should get counseling. He told my mother to take me to a psychiatrist because I was running away from home after Ortino left.

Then I stopped running away from home. Instead, I would leave at nine thirty or ten o'clock at night and go to the priests' house because Father McMahon was the only adult who knew what I had gone through that I could talk to. I couldn't talk to Monsignor Golina about this.

I would go to the rectory, ring the bell, and ask for Father McMahon. He would let me in and then he and I would sit in the parlor. I would have my head down and we would just sit there. I didn't even talk. But I went there because he knew.

My mother kept asking Father McMahon what she should do? He told her to take me to a psychiatrist. My mother asked him why? He replied, "Growing pains." That is how he explained it to her. Those were his very words. My mother told me this many years later.

I was twenty-three years old when I told my mother I had been raped by Ortino. Then I asked her if she would have believed me if I had told her I was being raped by a Catholic priest.

She replied that she probably would not have believed me because it was incomprehensible. It was unbelievable.

Ortino, before he left Painsville, had the audacity to call me at my house. My mother answered the phone, and handed it over to me. The phone was in the kitchen, so I couldn't leave the room. And my mother was standing right there. Ortino said, "I want you to meet me at the corner." We lived about half a block from a little tiny intersection. And he wanted me to meet him there.

I was terrified that he would come to our house. I knew I had to get out of the house. There was a friend, Johnny Barish was his name, and I played with him a lot. They were building new houses on the land where that intersection was. Johnny and I would often go into the construction areas at night and play. I was thirteen, but I was still a tomboy. I called Johnny and said let's go play in the basements. And we went over there.

I stood, looking out the basement window. And Ortino came. He drove around and around, looking for me. I don't know what Johnny Barish thought; I really have no idea. I would like to talk with him now and ask him. But I was obsessed with watching what was going to happen. Watching Ortino drive in circles, I could tell he was furious at me for not coming out to see him. Finally Ortino hit the gas, peeled some rubber off his tires, and took off.

Ortino called me a couple of times after that, asking me to meet him. But I wouldn't meet him. I didn't show up at the spots he would tell me to go. But that first time, I was terrified that he was going to come to the house.

After he left, he sent me two postcards. But just before he left, he called me at the house and said to me, "I can buy a trailer home and you can come with me. We will live in the trailer." This is what the guy said. He was whacko. He was really whacko. After what he had done to me and how I was acting toward him, he thought I was going to go live in a trailer with him?

It boggles my mind to look back at this and wonder where he was coming from. It was so bizarre, as if he was living in some fantasy world. How could he think I wanted any part of him? All he ever got from me was a negative response. I guess we all live in our own unique universe that give us the perceptions that we have. And his perception was off—way, way off.

I wish Father McMahon was still alive. I'm sure ready to hear what he has to say about what happened to me.

Recently, I have been involved with an organization called No More Secrets. It is supposed to deal with this abuse in the open and not have any more cover ups and secrets. Once at a scheduled meeting there were only three of us. Myself, a lay expert from the archdiocese, and a Catholic nun.

The three of use were talking about the moral actions that need to be taken by Archbishop Levada of San Francisco. At one point I gestured toward his picture hanging on the wall of the meeting room and said, "He's nothing but a CEO."

The other two women, official representatives of the Archdiocese of San Francisco, looked at each other and said, "She's got it!"

Then the three of us discussed how the Church is a business and they are treating this sexual abuse in a businesslike manner.

I listened, but thought back to the days when I was being raped by the priest that I had been taught was my direct connection to God and salvation. It wasn't a business to me.

Postscript

Sharan Falotico died on 24 October, 2003, shortly after telling her story for this book. Her death followed a lengthy period of time when she was dependent upon oxygen tanks for her normal breathing. Her physical condition was certainly affected by the nine months she spent in a psychiatric ward, her three suicide attempts, and the anger that literally consumed her body. Yet, though out all of her physical ordeals, her spirit remained strong and cheerful.

Victor Ortino was transferred to a monastery where he died five years later.

Luke's Story

Editor's Comments

Luke's story has many of the same features I heard from other survivors. When the priest started molesting him he had no one to turn to. His mother, a former nun, would never believe a priest could do anything wrong. His father, who had a fierce temper, was not in good health. Hearing news that his son was being molested by a priest could have triggered a fatal heart attack. Add to these factors the obligations Luke felt toward the priest as a man of God, and he was unable to terminate the relationship. The abuse continued for a period of more than four years.

Luke's story does show that the Church can take action on occasion. The bishop responsible for "Father Peter" asked him to take a lie detector test. He refused. Luke took, and passed, the lie detector test given by the police. The bishop defrocked Father Peter and removed him from all of his priestly duties.

Luke told me his story and gave me the true names of both the priest and his brother. However he has signed an agreement with the diocese not to reveal the names as part of the financial settlement he received.

We have identified the molesting priest simply as Father Peter.

Luke's brothers are not really named John and Joe.

I was molested by Father Peter, our parish priest, starting when I was fifteen years old. Father Peter was a long time family friend, who had been welcomed into our family life by my mother, a former nun, and my father and was considered a member of our family. This molestation continued from 1975 until 1979.

This friendship with our family, if it can be called that, with Father Peter started in the late sixties. Soon after he entered into our family life, he molested my older brother John. My older brother has never discussed this with me, but I am convinced he was molested by Father Peter before I was. My brother has also reached a legal and financial settlement with the diocese, but refuses to discuss this subject with me.

The molestation by Father Peter went from my brother to me and continued on through the early and mid-seventies. It finally came to an end when he tried to molest my younger brother. At this point, my mother and I brought it to the attention of the bishop.

I know the above covers several years, but I wanted to tell you the overview of my story. Now let me go back to the beginning and describe what actually took place.

My older brother John went to work for Father Peter at the church in the late sixties doing various things around the rectory and the church property—maintenance things. Father Peter took my brother on vacation to various places, such as Reno, Nevada. Several times they went to southern California. He took my brother to his brother's place down in the Los Angeles area. I forget exactly where—Canoga Park, or Thousand Oaks, or someplace like that. And I am sure there were other places he took him.

John and I are about the same size physically. We are both six feet tall and weighed about 180 pounds in high school—brown hair, glasses, sideburns. We both dressed mainly in Levi's and tried to stay up with the latest trends.

John seemed to have a good social life and he was well liked. We did not spend a lot of time together as he is six years older than me. That made me the pesky little brother, at least from my point of view.

John had several friends in high school. He seemed able to acquire and maintain friends easier than I did. He is still in contact with a few of them. Neither of us seemed to have any interest in playing sports.

Then Father Peter was reassigned to a parish in a town up north. There were no rumors of any abuse or any problems; it just seemed like a routine transfer. My brother followed him to do work for his new parish. Of course my parents and I were unaware of any sexual molestation at that time. My mother was just happy one of her sons was so close to the priest and working for the Church. And she was thrilled that the priest had actually offered John a job, to be working around the parish. John was only seventeen or eighteen.

We all adored Father Peter. We loved him. He had become such an integral part of our family and of our family life. He was simply a well liked man and a char-ismatic priest. And he paid attention to all of us and made us feel important to him.

Father Peter showered my brother with gifts. He bought him rings, watches, suits, and paid for part of his car. He wined and dined him, besides taking him on vacation. My parents thought this was wonderful, espe-cially my mother, a former nun. She believed Father Peter was a good role model, who would influence her son to live a priestly life. John was probably around fif-teen or sixteen when he started working for Father Peter, so he was a major role model, in my mother's eyes, on how to live a good Catholic lifestyle.

I don't know how John first started his relationship with Father Peter. We were both altar boys. John served as an altar boy for Father Peter, and I served as an altar boy for his successor. Of course our mother was always happy to see us as altar boys.

Later, when Father Peter returned to our city, I was to became a Eucharistic minister for him. He was very encouraging of me to become a Catholic priest. At one point, he blessed my hands, in a formal ceremony.

I was very envious of John at the time because he was getting all this attention from Father Peter, and of course, all the approval from our parents, and I was getting none.

Then in 1971, John broke off his relationship with Father Peter. He almost committed suicide. He tried to drive his car off a mountain road. I never spoke with my brother about this, and I don't know why he broke off his relationship with Father Peter. And since my parents never discussed this with me I never knew how, or if, he explained it to my parents. At that time, John was in a relationship with a woman; he was engaged to be married, and that fell apart for reasons I don't know. At any rate, he almost committed suicide. He ended up joining the military. While he was in the military, Father Peter returned to a parish in our city.

When Father Peter came back, he called my family. We welcomed him back with open arms. We were glad to have him back in town.

We moved from the parish we were living in over to Father Peter's new parish. The whole church was in disrepair. He needed somebody who could fix things. At that time, I was working with my dad on all of his rentals and I was quite handy, so I ended up working for him, fixing up his church, the rectory, and all that.

Father Peter had been ill previously with some type of liver disease—hepatitis or yellow jaundice or something. It had gone into remission prior to him coming back to town. That is why he was assigned there, because his illness was in remission. I never knew what had caused his illness, although he was a heavy drinker and heavy smoker. Father Peter never mentioned why he had gotten sick. I did know that he took several medications for his illness.

He had gotten ill one night, very ill. I guess he was having a relapse. It was suggested through the family that somebody needed to be there for him in case he needed to be rushed to the hospital or anything like that. Prior to all this, he had been showering me with gifts. He had been giving me watches and jewelry, supposedly that he got from his friend cheap.

I was playing chauffeur for him, driving his Mercury Marquis. He was taking me out to dinner and buying me suits. The restaurants he was taking me to were not cheap, they were some of the high class restaurants in town. Also, he took me to quite a few cocktail lounges.

The first night I stayed at the rectory to watch over him was event free, so this became a routine. A roll away bed was brought in for me. It was put into his bedroom, which was the only bedroom in the house.

I was there one night and heard him moaning in pain and agony. I went to comfort him. Now mind you, this was about 1975, mid-point of the year. I was about fifteen and one half years old.

I went to comfort him in his agony. I sat on the edge of his bed, or lounged on it, not quite laying down, but not quite sitting upright either. I ended up falling asleep. Later in the night I woke with his hand stroking my erect penis.

I had no idea what to do. This was a man of God, somebody I had loved. Somebody who was bringing me into salvation. I just froze, not knowing what to do. He masturbated me to climax, and that was that. I just lay there. I did get up later in the night and went to my own bed.

For the rest of the night, I thought of this. I was saying to myself, "My God, what just happened? What did I do?" I was in shock. I tried to erase it from my mind. This could not have happened. What is wrong with me? Am I going to Hell? I felt responsible and guilty for this abuse.

I continued to work for Father Peter, and he continued to sexually abuse me. Things occurred not only in town but down in Laguna Beach. He would frequently take me down there to a hotel on the beach. There were at least three occasions when he rented a hotel for a week and we would drive there. One year, he even rented a private home, to the tune of $750 a week. At that time, 1976 or 1977, that was a lot of money. And it was just him and I in this huge four- or five-bedroom house with a three car garage—the whole shebang.

When we were in Laguna Beach, I tried to stay down on the beach as much as possible. I got a few severe sunburns, but I became quite tan. I would be on the beach from early in the morning until either the sun went down or it was time for our dinner reservations.

We would dine at some very nice restaurants, such as André's, or the restaurants at the Surf 'n Sand Hotel.

One evening we had gone out to dinner and then went to a bar he wanted to go to. I was his chauffeur, so he directed me to this particular bar. It was a gay bar.

I was so ill at ease that all I remember about the interior is that it was dark. The bar stretched across most of the room; it was crowded, with men wall to wall, hanging on each other unabashedly. There was dancing, some slow dancing and then fast dancing. It didn't seem to matter to the men who were out there dancing. At one point Father Peter asked me to dance. I declined. I felt very uncomfortable being in that gay bar, gay men eyeballing me. I am not a homophobe, but I knew I was in the wrong place and did not want to be there.

The men in the bar were just ordinary gay men, some masculine, some feminine. No one extraordinarily flamboyant. I don't remember Father Peter knowing anyone in particular, although he seemed very comfortable in that type of environment. None of the bartenders or waitresses seemed to recognize Father Peter nor give him any special attention. I was just very, very uncomfortable with all of this. I didn't know what to think, didn't know what to do. I just wanted to get out of there. And of course I was still a minor at that time too.

So we left and went back to the rented house. This was a huge, modern home with several large fireplaces and high ceilings. I had already had quite a bit to drink, but I drove. At the time, I was drinking anything I could, just to numb the pain of my life. I drove back to the house and parked the car in the garage. We went into the house and up to the bedroom. He proceeded to have sex with me. Sometimes we had sex in the car, but only oral sex.

There are many details that I have blanked out of my mind. I think we slept in the same bed, but I am not sure. And I cannot remember every encounter. It seems every encounter involved a lot of drinking, and the details for many of these events are blurred by alcohol.

For lack of a better word, I have feelings of guilt and all that other stuff. Because I guess it can be viewed, and I often view it, as though I was a willing participant in the acts. I was a fifteen-year-old kid with these very strong feelings, and didn't know what to do with them. I was raised in a Catholic family so there wasn't much talk about sex or anything like that. I knew about homosexuality and I was very puzzled as to what was going on in my life. Here was a man who was supposed to be preaching against homosexuality performing these acts on me. It was quite a head trip. I cannot explain how confused I was, nor how confusing it was to me.

I wonder sometimes why I didn't stop working for him and being abused, but I had to. I was his chauffeur, his handy man. It just was not an option for me to leave.

Of course, this created a lot of problems for me in the other aspects of my life. At school I was attracted to girls, but I was afraid to get too close to them. I was scared they would find out what was happening to me by Father Peter and I couldn't deal with that threat, or even the thought of that threat.

I do have those qualms as to being a participant in those things. I have a lot of shame and a lot of guilt, or at least, I feel a lot of shame and a lot of guilt. I know in my head it was him; he is the one who should have all the shame and all the guilt. He is the one who crossed the line. I was a minor child. I know there cannot be consensual sex between an adult and a minor, especially if that adult is a Roman Catholic priest.

But, at the time, I was really confused by this sexual relationship I was forced into. There shouldn't be any sexualization of the relationship whatsoever because of the priest's celibacy. And that is one of the devastating things to me. I am violating a priest in his celibacy. I am making him go against his vows. And that is just totally devastating. It is as if I was leading a man into Hell, when it was quite the opposite. He was leading me into Hell, although he was supposed to be leading me into Heaven.

It takes a long, long time to come to grips with that kind of thing. I remember so many, many things and they all come rushing back at once. There was obviously sex in his bedroom. There was sex in the hotels. There was sex in his own brother's home down in Canoga Park, where he attempted to sodomize me. He ended up ripping me, not my rectum, but between the buttocks. I remember that every time I bathe. Because I feel it. It left scars, physical scars. Doctors have referred to it as a sinus. Basically that means it is a void. I have to make sure I keep it clean, especially during the summer, or otherwise it get infected. I don't mean to take you through the gruesome details, but I think people need to understand.

He did try to sodomize me several times. But I just remember this one specific time because it was painful. It is there for the rest of my life. There was oral sex. He performed oral sex on me and made me perform oral sex on him. Even today, almost twenty years later, it is very difficult for me to admit this and come to terms with it.

And he made me engage in a mutual masturbation type of thing with him. And he encouraged me to sodomize him. Which I attempted to do several times. How horrible, I just cannot describe how that feels.

Father Peter had a housekeeper. We often went over to her house for dinner and drinks and swimming because she had a pool. Of course, she cooked at the rectory for both of us. It sounds strange, but I don't think the housekeeper knew what was going on—or did not want to admit it to herself. Father Peter knew how to cover his tracks well. The housekeeper later accused me of making false allegations when I went to the bishop. But I never discussed what happened with the her. I knew she would not want to.

Father Peter had a friend in or near Irvine, who I thought was horribly gay, quite feminine. We would go to his place and stay there. I don't remember anything going on there because most of the time we were in separate bedrooms. I think he tried to hide our relationship from his gay friend.

This friend was a single man in a condominium house. He was very feminine and very vain. I don't know that he ever tried anything with anybody or not. I don't know if those two had sex or not. All I know is I was protected in my room by being in his house and being in a separate room.

I remember several times Father Peter complained that I never initiated sex, and he wanted to know why. Of course I couldn't tell him! How do you go against some-body like this? It was horrible being asked why I don't initiate sex. It was obvious. I didn't want it.

I was going to become a priest. He had convinced me. He had blessed my hands. I had become a Eucharist minister. I taught CCD in his parish. I was not just a maintenance man around there, I was damned near the assistant pastor. I didn't, obviously, administer any of the sacraments, but I was everywhere for that par-ish—midnight mass, everything. I distinctly remember one midnight mass on Christmas Eve. I had gone to a liquor store and purchased a bottle of Wild Turkey 101. And I was nearly sixteen years old. I wasn't carded. So I purchased it and took it back to the rectory. I started drinking before midnight mass. I ended up serving communion at mass. Later on, Christmas Day, I found out how much I had drunk of that bottle. Now mind you this was a quart bottle. There were only a few ounces left of it. I just drank myself into oblivion. I quite often did that. I wanted to numb my brain. Some psycholo-gists might call it self-medication, deadening the pain.

Whenever we would go out, we would go to the black-jack tables after dinner. I would sit there and drink and smoke cigarettes and play blackjack right along side of him. I was a mere sixteen years old.

And there is the one thing I remember apart from him, my social life apart from him. A lot of the kids at school called me fag. Faggot. Queer. I wondered what did they know? What did I show them? What was I doing that brought them to this conclusion? So I thought everybody thought I was gay. And I wasn't; I was just stuck in a situation I didn't know how to get out of.

One of the reasons I didn't try to get out of it was because my father, early in 1975, had open heart surgery—three bypasses, and he wasn't doing well. It didn't look like it was going to be as effective for him as it has been for other people. He subsequently died in 1979. So I knew that if I went and told my father, or if I told my mother, of course, my father would find out, it would lead to complications. Dad had quite a temper and I knew he would go and try to kill Father Peter. And he would end up dead from a heart attack himself.

I didn't dare tell anyone. And of course my mom was a nun before she met Dad. I remember thinking, "She is not going to believe me. There is no way she is going to believe me. Priests don't do that kind of thing, right?"

My mother had been a novice in a convent in Carmel, California. She was dismissed because she did not fit in. She felt the mother superior was not friendly to her. She thought it was because she has a deep voice, which was not what they wanted in the convent. They wanted a quieter person. One time she asked for a new bra as she was quite large and her old ones were worn. She was told not to be so vain and do without.

My mother was the one who brought Father Peter into our family. He was supposed to be a man of God, someone to lead us to salvation, just like the other priests that my parents befriended. Father Peter was not the first, but he was the closest. I think it is my mother's belief that she has to be a personal friend of her pastor as part her salvation requirements. She has always made it a point to befriend the parish priests and involve them in her family's life.

And she still looked up to the man herself. He could do no wrong. He forgave sins. He blessed the Eucharist. He anointed the sick and married people. He baptized people. How could somebody of that stature do such a thing? So I figured she would tell me I am wrong, I am imagining it. That I was the bad guy.

I had gone to the seminary for faith formation down in San Diego. I don't know exactly when I did that, but I graduated from high school in 1978 so it would have been either 1977 or 1978.

I didn't like what I was seeing down there. I didn't like it at all. There seemed to be too many gay men down there. I didn't see any sex going on, but it was just the atmosphere. So I decided, subconsciously, that was not for me. I was not going to be a priest. Later that year, I did tell my mom that I was not going to be a priest. I felt I was a sexual human being, and God wanted me to be that—to be a father, a real father.

At that point, I decided that since I was handy with my hands,and had taken four years of auto mechanics in high school, I would become an auto mechanic. At graduation from high school, I enrolled in Phoenix for an automotive technical school. I could have entered anytime after high school. I could have spent the summer goofing around, or doing whatever, a free life, and then in the fall go to Phoenix. But I choose to enter the school the month I graduated.

I went down to Phoenix and lived in an apartment with some guys. I had a job down there while I was going to school. Father Peter would come down to visit and invite me to stay in his hotel. Again, he would take me to the best of places in Phoenix, Trader Vic's in Scottsdale, the Arizona Biltmore for dinner. He spent hundreds and hundreds of dollars on dinners. And then he would take me back to the hotel and have his way with me.

In 1979, after completing that technical school, I was offered a job by his so-called nephew. His nephew worked for Granny Goose potato chips as a district manager. He needed another route man, so I went to selling potato chips. I even lived in this man's home with his wife and children. All of a sudden one day, my mother called me and asked me if Father Peter had touched me or did anything to me. Of course my initial response was "No, why, what is going on?"

My mother said he tried to molest Joe, my younger brother. I decided that was the end of it. He is not going to do this to anyone else, anywhere, no more. My mother later told me he did try with a couple other boys in the parish. I don't know when these incidents happened, or if they were before or after my brother Joe.

Father Peter had always told me it was love, and we had a special relationship. And it was OK with God. When he was trying it with somebody else, it blew all that right out the window. That can't be true. He can't love me if he is trying to do it with other boys. So I confessed to my mother, and she came up to Reno to see me.

We went to the bishop and spilled the beans. The bishop asked Father Peter if it was true, and asked him if he would take a lie detector test. Of course, the bishop also asked me if I would take a lie detector test. I agreed and went down to the Sheriff's station the next day. I took and passed the lie detector test.

Father Peter refused to take the test. He was defrocked. The bishop took him out of the parish and dismissed him from all of his duties. He retired him. He ended up on welfare in a retirement home.

But the son of a bitch had the audacity that, while all of this was going on and being revealed, before he was dismissed, to stand up at the pulpit in our parish church, while my mother was in the congregation, and say this crazy woman was making up these allegations against him. It was such a slap; it was unconscionable. I will never forget that, never. My mother has received death threats from other parishioners. Of course she had to leave that parish and go somewhere else. These so-called Christians, calling her up with death threats is bizarre, absolutely bizarre.

Years later, I had been thinking about my oldest brother. I had come to the conclusion that Peter had molested him prior to me. I remember trying to reconcile the two of them. I didn't know why they had had a falling out, but I knew the two of them were not talking any more. John came in to visit us from the military with his new wife. I called Father Peter and he consented to going out to dinner with all of us, so we did. That was that.

Years later I thought about him again. I had come to the conclusion that my brother had been molested by Father Peter, but I had no proof. And of course my brother would not talk to me about it, not that I would push the issue.

My brother and I met up in San Antonio one time and we had a short chat about that kind of thing, i.e., sexual molestation by a priest. He wouldn't acknowledge that he had been molested, but he acknowledged that he had been trying to defend himself against Father Peter, physically defend himself.

In 2000, I had been receiving some counseling and had been talking to my counselor. I concluded I should seek some recompense for this. At least they should be paying for counseling, if nothing else.

I had suffered a severe bout of depression in the early nineties and sought help from a psychiatrist. She recommended a psychologist. He took me through hypnosis, and we spoke briefly about me being raped by a priest. He tried to get me to talk about it openly, but I was not capable to speak of it. After I moved to California in 1998, I sought counseling for depression again. I have been in counseling ever since.

I called the diocese and asked them to pay for my counseling. They agreed. Monsignor Pat (not his true name) consented to paying for the counseling. But he wanted to know all the details. Of course he was just the administrator, he wasn't the bishop. A new bishop was coming in, and they didn't know who the new bishop would be. Of course my distrust of the Catholic Church was very high at the time. It still is. I consulted an attorney, telling him I didn't think I could trust the Church and this new bishop just coming in to agree to pay for my counseling. I decided to just ask for a lump sum. My attorney agreed.

He went to the attorneys the Church had at the time and said we wanted a lump sum. He had talked to the monsignor first, and the monsignor ended up turning it over to an attorney for the Church. They said if I wanted to receive anything I would have to file a lawsuit. I said "OK, you asked for it."

We filed a lawsuit for $2.2 million, and it was dismissed based on the statute of limitations since the acts were more than ten years old. In the state where we filed, the statute of limitations is very vague, and I was told that we could have won on appeal. In that state you go straight to the Supreme Court with your appeal. But because the court is so busy you have to go into mediation to see if you can resolve your differences there first.

We did all the paperwork and filed the appeal with the Supreme Court. We went into negotiations and the Church came to the table with an offer of $50,000. I laughed at them and said this is ridiculous and a slap in the face. It went on for the rest of the day until we were finally able to come to an agreement. Of course the attorneys took 40 percent of that.

My brother learned that I had sued the Church and asked me who my attorney was. I gave him the name of my attorney whom he retained and who was able to settle my brother's claim last Monday (Editor's note: November 4, 2002) for the same amount that I received. That makes me feel better.

Father Peter is dead. I am sure in some spiritual way he is paying the price, but he never paid the price here on earth. He died in 1983. Before he died, I did go back to see him. I found out where he was living and I knocked on his door. I confronted him. He was ever so congenial and so Christian, so forgiving. But he still maintained that he did nothing wrong, because it was love. I walked out and left it at that. I never saw the man again.

I don't know exactly what he died of, but last year I found out from the local authorities that he died of "natural causes." For years I lived in fear of AIDS. Thankfully, the military routinely tests for AIDS, and I spent a number of years on active duty. I used to donate blood, which involves a blood test, just to find out if there was anything wrong with my blood.

I wondered if my mother would continue to see him, especially after the bishop had defrocked him and he was living in a retirement home on welfare. Recently I was told by a former neighbor that my mother continued to visit him and to help him out.

I have thought about this and how it affected my mother and her faith in the Catholic Church. She has asked me for forgiveness and still does sometimes. She continues to attend daily mass when possible. I asked her recently why she does. She told me she does so to ask for forgiveness.

Throughout the entire three years that I was living with Father Peter and being abused, there were several things that should have sent signals to a lot of people. I think they just ignored the signals.

I was ordered to call him by his first name, or his nickname, Pete. Amongst the immediate parishioners it was supposed to be Father Peter, but around other people it was to be Uncle Pete. Especially in the general public it was to be Uncle Pete.

That should have been a signal to people who knew him as a priest. I don't know, I just think it should have been a signal. It was quite often what happens, they have you call them Uncle to explain why an older man is spending so much time with a younger man.

I do remember his nephew, his supposedly real nephew, Bill, living up there in Reno, only he was actually Father Peter's son. Father Peter told me he had previously been married and widowed; his wife died in childbirth, and that he gave up his son for adoption to his sister. Of course I have never talked to anybody else about this, to confirm it or anything. But everybody there called him Uncle Pete. Bill's family, his wife, his kids and Bill, Jr. They all called him Uncle Pete. I have often wondered if Bill had been abused.

This priest had been a priest for twenty-five years by the time he caught up with me. So he had served in several parishes before. One was at a Catholic high school where he was the principal. He would have had access to a lot of kids. But I am not aware of any reports of abuse there. Of course, there is no reason I would have known about any abuse there.

Father Peter was also assigned to a parish out in a remote town. So he had plenty of access to other kids elsewhere. I often wonder what other kids he did get. I know in my heart that my brothers and I were not the first nor the only ones. It doesn't happen like that.

I hope to God I was the last. But I doubt that. I think he did touch somebody else. I hope and pray they weren't touched as much as I was. It could still be devastating; even once can be devastating. Totally devastating. I know it has been for a lot of guys.

That is basically my story.

Unfortunately I signed a confidentiality agreement with the diocese and I cannot provide any documentation or tell you exactly what amount I settled for. When my brother settled his lawsuit, he did not have to sign a confidentiality agreement. But my brother will not talk to you and won't discuss this at all.

If I could do anything to help others, it would be to urge people to watch out for the signals of abuse. I feel there were many signals that I was being abused that the people around Father Peter ignored. I was accused by a parishioner of shacking up with him. Bingo, right there! A big old clue. Somebody ought to know that, if I am shacking up with a priest, there is something wrong here and they should say something to somebody.

Just the fact that I was around so often should have been a clue that something was wrong. Why are this boy's parents allowing him to hang around here so much? Why is this boy going on vacation with this priest? Why so much preferential treatment with this one particular boy?

I think the molestation, as far as the boys in our family, ended with me. Father Peter tried to molest my younger brother Joe, but he failed. My younger brother Joe is kind of a redneck. He gets very angry. So I don't think he will talk very much even if he was molested. From what I understand of his situation, Father Peter's legs were hurting one day, or one evening, and he asked my brother Joe to massage them. And so he did. Father Peter was laying on his belly at first, and then he rolled over and he had an erection. My brother asked him what was going on with that. Father Peter replied that it was a natural thing, and it occurs naturally. My brother left. He thought something was wrong and so he left. When he got home, he told my mother, and that is when the molestations came to light. Joe is two years younger than I am, so he would have been sixteen or seventeen years old at that time.

And that is my story. I wish no one else will ever have this type of story to tell. But I am afraid there are many other stories of abuse like mine.

If you would like to purchase additional copies of this book call:

Tapestry Press
3649 Conflans Road
Suite 103
Irving, TX 75061
www.tapestrypressinc.com

877-920-8856

If you would like to:

► *contact the editor of this book with comments about it*

► *discuss your own story of abuse*

Go to the following web site:

www.survivorspress.com